My Birding Life

Moss Taylor (signature)

Moss Taylor

Other books by Moss Taylor

The birds of Sheringham (1987)
The Birds of Norfolk (1999 with Michael Seago, Don Dorling &
      Peter Allard)
Guardian Spirit of the East Bank (2002)
In the Countryside (2003)
Collins Identifying Birds by Colour (2008 with Norman Arlott)
The Norfolk Bird Atlas (2011 with John Marchant)
My Family Through Six Generations (2015)
Wings over Weybourne (2018)
Rare and Scarce Birds in North-east Norfolk (2019)

Cover photograph – The author (*Chris Taylor*)

ISBN 978-0-9542545-8-2
First published 2020 by Wren Publishing, Sheringham, Norfolk
Printed in Great Britain by Swallowtail Print of Norwich, Norfolk
Copyright Moss Taylor 2020

Contents

This book is dedicated to

Robina Churchyard,

my birding companion and soulmate

for the last 13 years.

Introduction and Acknowledgements

The great advantage of writing your autobiography is that the research needed brings back an enormous number of happy memories that might otherwise have been forgotten forever. This is particularly so, when the book is devoted to a lifelong hobby, such as birdwatching. As Richard Porter states in his generous Foreword, this book dwells on only one aspect of my life, my family and working life having been covered in an earlier book *My Family Through Six Generations*.

I have been particularly fortunate throughout my life in having lived in areas that have allowed me to follow my great interest in the natural world. Initially in metropolitan Essex in the 1950s before the area became urbanised, and then for the greater part of my adult life in the wonderful, rural county of Norfolk. During this time I have been lucky enough to meet and befriend many other people with a similar interest, some of whom I still know from my earliest days at Chigwell School. Together we have had many enjoyable birding trips away both in England and abroad. I would also like to add my sincere gratitude to Sir Michael Savory, the owner of Weybourne Camp, who has allowed me unrestricted access to what I have called 'My Spiritual Home' for at least the last 20 years.

For many years I have enjoyed writing about my exploits in the field and this autobiography is unusual in that it incorporates many of the articles that I have had published in local and national birdwatching journals. For permission to include them or extracts from them, I am most grateful to the editors or officers of the following magazines and organisations: Bardsey Bird Observatory, *Birdwatch*, *Bird Watching* (www.birdwatching.co.uk), *British Birds*, British Trust for Ornithology, Cley Bird Club, Cumberland Bird Observers Club Inc, Eastern Counties Newspapers, *Just Sheringham*, Neotropical Bird Club, Norfolk & Norwich Naturalists' Society, *Norfolk Bird Report*, *Norfolk Natterjack*, North East Norfolk Bird Club and Poppyland Publishing.

All the photos in the book were taken by me unless credited to another photographer, and I am most grateful to Peter Allard, Jeremy Bagnall-Oakeley, Robina Churchyard, Tim Davis, Sue Goldsmith, Stanley Howe, Antony Kelly, Pete Morris and Chris Taylor (christaylorphoto.co.uk) for allowing me to use their photographs. I am particularly indebted to my son, Chris, who took the photo for the front cover and to my son, Nik, for his design of the front cover. I extend my thanks to my partner Robina Churchyard, who kindly read through the early drafts of each chapter and made some most useful comments (*most* of which have been incorporated!). I am most grateful to Mike Dawson and his team at Swallowtail Print for all their help in the production of this book. Finally, but not least, I would like to express my sincere gratitude to Richard Porter for agreeing to write the Foreword to this book, which I have little doubt will boost the sales.

All profits from the sale of the book will be going to our charity Love for Leo that helps to finance equipment and treatment, which is not available under the National Health Service, for Norfolk and Suffolk children with cerebral palsy. Further details are given at the end of the book.

Moss Taylor
September 2020

Foreword

When you pass your allotted three score years and ten, such a history as *My Birding Life* starts to take on a meaning probably more relevant than to a young birder yet to earn his spurs. Looking back over our privileged post-war years, reflecting and reminiscing about the good old days with friends - we must pinch ourselves to remind us how lucky we are in Britain and the western world to be able to so indulge.

This book is essentially an autobiography of those years, though it dwells on only one aspect of the author's life – that of a birdwatcher. Birdwatcher? Well I think ornithologist would be more appropriate. Moss Taylor has crammed into the 70 years that his book covers as much serious ornithology as would many a professional. And on top of this he has had a long career as a General Practitioner, as well as being a caring husband, father and grandfather who plays golf, has a deep interest in history and is a renowned host.

This book presents an eclectic mix of the life of a highly respected birder who has witnessed the myriad developments in ornithology since the 1950s. Norfolk features prominently as this has been Moss's spiritual home for much of his life and his great contribution to the county comes through the pages of his book. Many tales and stories revolve around his adopted county.

You will hear about his love affair with meticulous note keeping, his obsession with ringing, his travels, his passion for the BTO, his writing and, of course, his need to be in the field watching birds – and finding rarities. There are birding intrigues, tales of suppression, spats, rivalry. The legendry Nancy's Café and Richard Richardson have their allotted slots.

When you consider how the popularity of birding has grown since the mid-20th century I find it surprising that there are so few books about the lives of birders - personal accounts through the eyes of a gifted writer. So I know that *My Birding Life* will, deservedly, have an important place in the annals of our hobby.

Richard Porter,
Cley next the Sea, September 2020

Chapter 1

From nestling to fledging

Traditionally, autobiographies by birders are told as tales of their exploits in the British Isles and further afield. Two of my favourites are H.G.Alexander's *Seventy Years of Birdwatching*, which covers his early birdwatching years from 1897 and takes us on a fascinating trip through the first two-thirds of the 20th century, describing the developing study of ornithology at home and abroad. The other is *Beguiled by Birds* by that doyen of 20th century ornithology, Ian (D.I.M.) Wallace. Like Horace Alexander, Ian describes the course of British birdwatching but from the 17th century up to the start of the 21st century, in particular the 'golden years' of the 1970s and 1980s. His text is enlivened by many of his own delightful watercolours and a wealth of historic photographs. It's the sort of book that can be read and re-read many times.

Whereas my birding autobiography covers the 70 years of my obsession with birds and addiction to the written word, from the 1950s up to the end of the second decade of the 21st century. It has been written as a means of communicating excerpts from some of my books, articles and newspaper columns, to a wider readership – hopefully readers will enjoy them as much as I have enjoyed writing them. It also gives me the opportunity to describe the dramatic and far-reaching changes that have taken place in optical and photographic equipment, in field guides and in the means of disseminating bird information during the last 50 years.

Like many children growing up in the 1950s, my first bird identification book was *The Observer's Book of Birds*, although my interest in natural history probably started in the late 1940s when I was only five, as I explained in *My Family Through Six Generations*:

> Many of my earliest books concerned the natural world. In fact it may well have been two books that I received as prizes in 1948 and 1949 for 'Attendance and Good Conduct' at the Brixton Hill Methodist Church Sunday School, entitled respectively *The Billy Beaver Book* and *Peter the Puffin*, that started the ball rolling.

My Prize for 'Attendance and Good Conduct' in 1949.

One of my Christmas presents in 1951 was *Nature Rambles* by Edward Step, while the following year I was given *Wild Flowers at a Glance*, in which the flowers were innovatively arranged by colour (an invaluable aid to identification for a nine-year old) and *The Observer's Book of Birds*, the first of many in the series that I added to my ever-growing collection of natural history books.

While living in Brixton in the late 1940s, one of my favourite walks was around Brockwell Park, a typical municipal park with swings and roundabouts, extensive areas of mown grass and a large pond. But despite still being at infant school, it wasn't the playground that especially attracted me, but rather the pond, where I was never happier than when watching and feeding the motley collection of ducks, predominantly Mallards and Khaki Campbells. The latter is probably a variety of Mallard that is unknown to the majority of present-day birders, but was particularly common in the London Parks in the 1940s and 50s. It was the colour of milky coffee with a dark brown speculum. It was even illustrated and described in *The Pocket Guide to British Birds* by Fitter and Richardson, first published in 1952.

In 1950 my father, Albert Taylor, who was a dispensing chemist, was offered a partnership in an expanding business in Essex, and so as a seven-year old I moved from the grime and smoke of London to the Essex countryside, for in those days it really was rural, even in the Metropolitan part of the county. Despite the fact that we had moved to Harold Hill, a new council estate, there were still plenty of open fields and woods for me to explore, often alone, which in those days caused no concern to youngsters' parents. How different things are today and how lucky we were to have grown up in 'safer' times. After three years of living in the flat above Dad's chemist shop, we moved to a semi-detached property overlooking a large grassy field adorned with a myriad of wild flowers, bordered by unmanaged hedgerows and next to an area of mixed woodland, an absolutely perfect setting for my burgeoning interest in natural history.

Like many birders and naturalists of my generation, I initially relied on the excellent series of *Observer's Books* to identify the butterflies and wild flowers, as well as the birds, which I came across on my frequent sorties into the surrounding countryside. Again like many youngsters in the 1950s, I started to collect birds' eggs, although I never took more than one from any clutch. I would pierce a small hole in both ends of the egg, using a thorn, and then the contents would be blown out through one of the holes. However, things did not always work out as expected and I can well remember blowing an addled Song Thrush's egg, which clearly had been taken from a long-deserted nest, and the subsequent smell of rotten eggs almost put me off taking any more!

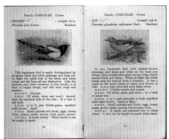

Opening pages in my *Observer's Book of Birds*.

2

The 1950s also saw the launch of the series of *I-Spy books* in association with the national newspaper the *News Chronicle*. The first one to be printed in colour was *I-Spy Birds* and this was soon added to my rapidly growing collection of natural history books. The booklet included descriptions and pictures of 71 common British birds, each one worth from 15 to 30 points depending on its abundance. I still have my original *I-Spy Birds* and it is interesting to note that whereas the sighting of a Great Spotted Woodpecker warranted 25 points, a Cuckoo was only worth 20, such have been the changing fortunes of these two species over the years. My first entry was a Barn Owl recorded on Dartmoor, while on our annual summer holiday, on 18th August 1953. By 1957, I had seen enough species and scored sufficient points (1,000) for the book to be sent to Big Chief I-Spy at the *News Chronicle* Wigwam in London, to apply for my 2nd class certificate and a feather to wear in my Red Indian headband. This was awaited with great anticipation and I can still remember the long brown envelope arriving through the post, but imagine my disappointment on opening it, to discover that the reward for achieving the 'Tribal Rank of Bird Spotter (2nd class)' was a pink feather! In case you are wondering, no, I never did wear it.

My original *I-Spy Birds*.

Undoubtedly one of the most important events in my birding life was when I started as a boarder in the junior house, Grange Court, at Chigwell School in Essex, in September 1954. Being an only child, I was really looking forward to living with other boys of my age, hoping that I would find some with a similar interest in natural history. I was not disappointed, for in my class and dormitory was Richard Collins, who was also a keen birdwatcher and over the years at school we spent many happy hours together exploring the 40 acres of school fields. Like me, on leaving school Richard became a medical student in London and went on to become a most successful vascular surgeon at the Kent & Canterbury Hospital. I was delighted at the start of my second term when another enthusiastic and far more knowledgeable birdwatcher, Mike Bowtell, also became a pupil at Chigwell and we became firm friends, a friendship that has lasted for over 65 years. It was Mike that first introduced me to the importance of learning bird songs as an additional means of identifying them, and later to the rewards of trapping and colour ringing birds. Richard, Mike and I would spend much of our free time in the summer, searching for birds' nests in the copses, hedgerows and grassy banks around the edges of the playing fields, keeping careful records of clutch size and fledging success. By this stage I had stopped the practice of egg collecting, although it was still not illegal, and I gave my collection to the biology department at the school.

Another very influential boy at Chigwell, who was several years older than us, was David Gordon, who was a far more experienced birdwatcher and he honed our skills in identifying birds, and also introduced us to the delights of watching waders and wildfowl, in addition to garden and woodland birds. He also impressed on us the importance of keeping careful records of the species we saw. While one of the English masters at the school was David Ballance, who later co-authored with Eileen Palmer *The Birds of Somerset*, and he too was a very positive influence on our growing interest in birds.

In my second year, much to my amazement, I came top of the class; equally surprised was my housemaster, Arnold Fellows, who told my parents that it wasn't likely to be repeated and how right he was! For my form prize, which I received on Speech Day, I chose Fitter & Richardson's *Collins Pocket Guide to Nests and Eggs*. Little did I know at the time that one day I would become a good friend of the artist Richard Richardson, and even write and publish his biography in 2002, as well as writing a book on bird identification myself for the same publishing house.

Form Prize, IVB

Presented to : M.P.Taylor

Speech Day : 1956   DHThompson
                      Headmaster

Entry in Fitter & Richardson's *Collins Pocket Guide to Nests and Eggs*.

In the 1950s, all published records in county bird reports, including even the commoner species, were followed by the initials of the observer, and I was thrilled when my sighting of a male Black Redstart on 15th April 1958 on Harold Hill duly appeared in the *Essex Bird Report* alongside my initials. Understandably this tradition had been discontinued by the early 1960s, as the number of records submitted to county recorders increased dramatically.

BLACK REDSTART

The passage of this species was perhaps the outstanding feature of the spring. Details are as follows:—Walton/Naze, 1-2 on many dates between March 27th and April 22nd (SCo, JAF, PP, CSS, JKW *et al.*); Bradwell, one on March 31st and April 2nd and two on the 12th and 16th (BBO); Foulness I., 1-2 on seven dates between March 25th and April 19th (MAA, GF, RHud, NP, PR *et al.*); single birds were reported from Leewick on March 28th and April 8th/9th (SCo, MSJS); E. Mersea on March 30th/31st and April 3rd (MRC, RHar, RL, CFM); Rowhedge on April 4th (*per* AEV); S. Benfleet on the 5th (GE); Landermere on the 6th (ATN, CSS *et al.*); Layer-de-la-Haye (SCo, RJM, SM) and Flatford (AH) on the 7th; Nazeing on the 8th/9th (BHK); Colchester (Shrub End) on the 13th (MSJS); Clacton (*per* KMA) and Harold Hill (MPT) on the 15th; and Abberton R. on the 22nd (JWA).

Autumn/winter records (of single birds in all cases):—Girling R., Chingford, August 17th (JCE) and September 17th (BSM); Little Clacton, September 5th (SCo); Bradwell, October 19th (BBO); Leewick, 27th (ALB); Naze, November 8th (MSJS); St. Osyth, December 10th (RWA).

My first published record: a Black Redstart in 1958.

Later that same year, David Gordon took Richard Collins and me to Goldhanger, for our first bird-watching visit to the Essex coast. The date was 28th December 1958, and it was a memorable day as I recorded no fewer than 12 lifers, albeit common species, such as Shelduck, Turnstone and Rock Pipit, as well as a pair of Scaup. It was also the start of my first birding notebooks, which have continued, without a break, ever since. Over the next 27 years, my records filled no fewer than 21 hand-written books, since when eight folders have held my computer-generated printed records, with hopefully many more yet to come. In addition I have amassed 27 Ringing Logs and 60 Field Note Books. But what will become of them after I have gone? This was a question that I posed in the journal *British Birds* in April 2015, a problem that will face many birders of my generation and one that has not yet been satisfactorily answered.

It was on one of my annual visits to stay with Mike Bowtell that he first introduced me to the thrill of trapping and colour ringing garden birds, in order to study the local population. In those days catching and colour ringing birds was totally uncontrolled and no licence or training was required. The rings were obtained by post from Greenrigg in Woodford Green. By 1959, Mike and his parents had moved from Braintree to High Garrett, where he had started to trap and colour ring the tits, finches and Blackbirds that were frequent visitors to his garden. By using unique colour combinations, he was able to identify the birds individually. On returning home to Gidea Park, to where we had moved in 1957, I tried catching Starlings by using an upturned garden sieve supported by a stick, which could be pulled away by a length of string. However, I had soon made a proper wire Potter trap along the lines of those used by Mike, and began to catch and colour ring tits and finches myself. One can imagine my excitement, when on 16th December 1959, I trapped my first BTO-ringed Greenfinch, a male that had been ringed a couple of miles away in Romford two years earlier. I was now hooked, and within a few months had made my first visit to Romford Ringing Station based at the local sewage farm, where I started training the following year as a BTO bird ringer. As they say, the rest is history!

Species	Age when Ringed Pull. = nestling	Sex ♂ = male, ♀ = female.	Ring Number
Greenfinch	full-grown	♂	V 27.035

	Date	Place	Co-ordinates
Ringed	16.2.57	Romford (Essex)	
Recovered	16.12.59	Gidea Park, Romford	
Movement	Local		18 Dec.59
Recovery Details	Caught, presumed released.		
Ringer	Hurrell & Waite		
Finder	M. Taylor, 24 Links Avenue, Gidea Park.		BRC.1B

My first ringing recovery.

It was also while I was at Chigwell School that I had my first bird article published. It appeared in *The Chigwell School Natural History Magazine* in 1961. The magazine ran to 24 pages and contained articles by ten members of the Natural History Society reflecting their particular interests. These covered topics as diverse as

'Fossil collecting in the Lyme Regis area', 'On the rearing of silk worm moths' and beekeeping, under the clever title of 'The beehiveiour of bees'. My short contribution was on 'The nesting of birds in the school grounds' and of interest I commented that "Tree Sparrows seem to be getting commoner in the grounds, and several pairs nested in the past few years." However, the most comprehensive article was by my friend, Mike Bowtell, on 'Colour ringing garden birds', which was the winning entry for the Natural History Prize Essay. Little did I realise at the time that my short piece would be the start of a lifelong interest in putting pen to paper.

Cover of *The Chigwell School Natural History Magazine*.

* * *

Chapter 2

Early days as a ringer

There is no doubt that bird ringing can be as addictive as alcohol and drugs, as I found out shortly after my initial visits to Romford Ringing Station. I well remember on my first visit on 16th April 1960, being shown a Meadow Pipit in the hand and being asked to identify it. I hadn't a clue and think I suggested that it might be a Dunnock. A fortnight later and on the day before term started I returned to the ringing station and couldn't wait for the summer holidays to begin, when I could once again examine birds in the hand and watch them being ringed. As I was still a boarder at Chigwell School studying for my 'A' Levels, my visits were limited to the school holidays. At last, August arrived and I cycled down to the sewage farm, eager to get involved as a British Trust for Ornithology (BTO) ringer. At that time the ringing station was run by two of the most respected ringers in the county: Bob Spencer and Fred Trust. Bob was not only a very keen and competent ringer and ringing trainer, but was also the head of the BTO Bird Ringing Scheme, with the title of Ringing Officer, having taken over from Miss Elsie Leach in 1954. In those days, the 'Ringing Office' was a single room in that section of the Natural History Museum in South Kensington known as the Bird Room. By September 1963 the BTO had moved to Beech Grove in Tring, Hertfordshire, and Bob moved from his home in Upminster to Tring, and so no longer ringed at Romford Ringing Station. On his move, Fred Trust took over the task of organising the ringing and training of new ringers at Romford. He was ideally suited for this role having himself been trained by Bob, while his professional work was as Deputy Chief Officer for the London Fire Brigade. A strict disciplinarian, Fred ensured that the very high standards introduced by Bob were maintained, and the work and output of the Romford Ringing Station went from strength to strength.

By the end of the school holidays I had convinced Bob and Fred that I really had the enthusiasm to undergo the strict training needed to become a BTO ringer, and on 17th September 1960 I was allowed to ring my first birds: a Yellow and a Pied Wagtail, as well as extracting the Yellow Wagtail from a mist net, a task even more difficult than the ringing and measuring of the bird. Thus I started on a path that I would follow for the next 55 years.

Although in those days, it was officially only necessary to ring 50 birds to obtain a 'C' permit, which allowed one to ring birds unsupervised, in practice Bob and Fred wisely insisted that far more experience was needed and those of us who were fortunate enough to be trained at Romford had usually ringed in excess of 500 birds before being passed for a 'C' permit. Having left school at the end of the summer term in 1961, I was able to spend far more time ringing at Romford Ringing Station, particularly as a I had failed one of my 'A' Levels and so in effect had a 'Gap Year' before starting at Medical School. I was also fortunate to be taken under the wing of Colin Carter, another ringer trained at Romford and living in the area, who I accompanied on ringing trips to South Ockendon Gravel Pits for *Acrocephalus* warblers (in recent years the very same pits have been managed by the Essex Wildlife Trust as the Chafford Gorges Nature Park). We also regularly ringed at a mixed thrush and finch roost in a rhododendron copse at Weald Park.

All this enabled me to obtain my 'C' permit in the spring of 1962, and by early August I had progressed to an 'A' permit, allowing me to use my own rings and find my own ringing sites, although I continued to ring at Romford Ringing Station for another two years. By the end of 1964, almost 59,000 birds of 83 species had been ringed at this inland site since it was first established by Bob Spencer in 1954. One of the most successful methods of catching the birds was the use of the small, wire Ottenby wader traps baited with mealworms and shredded coconut, and set on the dried out settling beds and surrounding fields. Amongst the impressive ringing totals were 1,500 Skylarks (a species rarely ringed elsewhere in Britain as adults), 3,000 Meadow Pipits, 2,000 Pied Wagtails and 3,700 Tree Sparrows. But the ringing station was best known for the netting of Sand Martins as they flew along the River Rom in late summer and autumn. However, it was not without its potential dangers, as we needed to wade in the water up to our waists to extract the birds from the mist nets, and the treated effluent from the sewage farm was discharged directly into the river. Just how none of us ever caught Weil's disease, amazes me, for we frequently encountered rats while ringing! It was well worth the effort though, as over 6,000 Sand Martins were ringed and it spawned the BTO Sand Martin enquiry.

I shall always remember the thrill of catching a juvenile Swallow in a mist net set along a hedgerow at West Mersea in Essex on 15th August 1962, the first bird that I was able to ring using my own rings – the first of over 66,500 over the course of the next 50 years. Back in those days, one of the main reasons for ringing birds was to discover their migration routes and the wintering areas of our summer migrants. However, the recovery rate for passerines was extremely low and as a rule many hundreds needed to be ringed, in order to be rewarded with a single foreign recovery.

Naturally my nets and rings accompanied me on a two-week holiday to Watermouth in North Devon at the end of August, where we stayed in a caravan on a farm. Not long after our arrival my nets were up and I started to catch the local Swallows and wagtails, including a Grey Wagtail, a new species for my ringing list. But what turned out to be the most exciting bird of the trip, was a Pied Wagtail, only the 50th bird I had ringed with my own rings, which was subsequently found four months later in Portugal. Sadly, it had been killed by a hunter, which even to this day is still a common fate for many of our migrants that winter or pass through Iberia.

Back in Essex, I started to ring at a gravel pit at Newbury Park, where Reed and Sedge Warblers were the main targets, although two Nightingales that turned up in the nets were a nice bonus. In 1963, I also joined the ringing rota at Bradwell Bird Observatory. Being situated on the coast at the mouth of the River Blackwater, the ringing thicket attracted good numbers of autumn migrants and during the weekend of my first visit in August a total of 22 species was ringed, which included a Wood Warbler. Unbeknown to me at the time it was only the second Wood Warbler to have been ringed at Bradwell. Having satisfied myself that I had correctly identified it, I duly ringed and measured it, before taking it along to Linnet's Cottage, the Bird Observatory's headquarters to show it to Malcolm Chettleburgh and Alan Old, two of the Bradwell stalwarts. They were not best pleased that I had already placed a ring around its leg, as neither of them had Wood Warbler on their personal ringing lists! This was the start of my love of ringing birds on migration, but little did I know then that one day I would be living on the north Norfolk coast and establishing two very successful coastal ringing sites.

Having started at medical school in London in October 1962, my free time was obviously limited, but never-the-less I still managed to ring over 1,500 birds most years, the vast majority at Weald Park, during my weekend visits to my parents in Essex. I was still in touch with Bob Spencer, who had trained me at Romford Ringing Station, and much to my surprise he asked me if I would like to join him on a BTO ringing trip to Morocco in spring 1965, as the expedition's medical officer. At the time I was only just beginning to start my clinical attachments and had examined very few patients, let alone prescribe any medication or administer an injection! Knowing that this would mean being away from my studies for about a month, I approached the Head of the Biochemistry Department, Professor Lawson, who I knew was a keen ornithologist himself. You can imagine my delight, when he informed me that the Dean, Dr Frances Gardiner, had agreed to let me go, with the proviso that I would write up my adventures in *The Royal Free Hospital Journal*. I needed no second invitation and an extract from the account of our trip follows:

The title page of the article with a photograph of the author (*anon*).

… The party consisted of eight people, being jointly led by John Ash, director of The Game Research Institute at Fordingbridge, a first-class field ornithologist, and Johnnie Johnson, one of the outstanding bird photographers of the present time. Also in the party were Bob Spencer, Cyril Walker (who worked in the palaeontology department at the Natural History Museum, London), Steve Boddy, Gwen Johnson and Christopher Headlam.

The expedition members from left to right: John Ash, the author, Cyril Walker, Gwen & Johnnie Johnson, Steve Boddy, three French ringers and Christopher Headlam (second from right).

We set off from London on March 25th and flew to Gibraltar, arriving there at about midnight. We were greeted with the news that the La Linea border into Spain was closing in twenty minutes. After a rather anxious period waiting for our bags to be unloaded from the plane, we were hurried through customs and just reached the Spanish border as it was closing.

Once into Spain, we were met by two other members of the party, Johnnie and Gwen Johnson from the Channel Islands who had earlier driven down to Spain and were waiting for us with their car. From here we drove to Malaga, a Spanish port on the Mediterranean coast, from where we were to sail the next day to Melilla in Morocco. We left Malaga in the evening on board a ship that I hardly would have trusted to take me across the Thames, let alone the Mediterranean. However, we awoke the following morning to find that we were still afloat and in sight of the African coast.

We landed at Melilla soon after eight and before long we were driving south through northern Morocco, passing many vineyards and orange groves, the trees laden with fruit. The last large town we came to was Oujda, where we stocked up with provisions for the next three weeks. The bird life now changed considerably and for the first time we were seeing species characteristic of North Africa, such as Brown-necked Ravens, Red-tailed Wheatears and Desert Horned Larks, as well as a loose flock of 400 Wheatears.

Continuing south we entered the true desert, a great cloud of sand arising from behind the car as we drove along. Eventually we sighted the oasis ahead that was to become our 'home' for the next three weeks. Defilia Oasis, as it is known, is situated in the middle of a valley about seven miles wide with mountains arising on either side. Along the middle of the valley flows a small river, or wadi, no more than 40 feet across at its widest point. At one end of the oasis was a palmery and leading along from this for about three-quarters of a mile were oleander bushes, lining the banks of the wadi.

We set up camp in the palmery, Cyril Walker and I sleeping in a tent and Johnnie and Gwen in their motent, a small caravan with a folding canvas roof, which we had been towing behind the car. One of the objects of the trip was to ring migrant birds, which were to be caught in fine nets, known as mist nets that varied in length from 20 to 60 feet. About 50 of these were erected across the river and between the oleander bushes.

By the next morning we were fully operational and began to catch the first birds for ringing. The very first one that we took from the nets was a fine male Collared Flycatcher, a species that had never before been recorded in Morocco, although over the course of the next three weeks we caught six more. We also caught a magnificent male White-spotted Bluethroat, the first of eight that we ringed during the trip.

On April 3rd the first big fall of birds occurred, no doubt due to the overnight change in the weather. It was now overcast and much cooler, whereas during the previous days it had been cloudless and almost unbearably hot. During the day we estimated that 3,000

Swallows passed through the oasis, 100 Nightingales and 300 Yellow Wagtails, as well as a River Warbler that we ringed, another new species for Morocco. The overcast weather continued the next day and an even greater fall of migrants occurred, and we ringed 619 birds of an even wider range of species. Six of the Sand Martins that we trapped were already bearing rings, four that had been ringed in Britain (including one that was taken out of a mist net by Steve Boddy that he had ringed himself in England!) and one each from Germany and Holland.

River Warbler, the first record for Morocco.

So far we had had a most successful trip, in our first five days we had ringed just over 1,300 birds of 41 species. Unfortunately disaster overtook us during the night of April 5th. The day had been overcast again and the migrants were still passing through in fairly good numbers. We had ringed just over 200 birds, including a Black-winged Stilt, a most dainty bird in the field but extremely ungainly in the hand. In the evening we noticed that some ugly black clouds were building up to the west of us and were moving very quickly in our direction. It began to rain at about nine o'clock and as we had pitched our tent near to the river, we moved it to some higher ground in case the water in the wadi should rise.

Black-winged Stilt netted for ringing.

Believing there to be no real danger from the rain we turned in at about ten o'clock and were soon fast asleep. Just after midnight, we were awoken by Johnnie telling us that the rain had continued and the wadi had risen considerably and was well over its banks. Apparently Johnnie and Gwen, who were sleeping in the motent, had been woken by a jolt and on jumping out of their bunks found that there were six inches of water inside. Not being able to find a torch, they had leapt outside to discover to their horror that both the car and motent were afloat, although they had parked at least ten feet above the normal level of the river. The bump that had awoken them was the motent being washed against the side of the car.

Now fully awake, I could hear the roar of the flooded river as it rushed madly along. We dressed and went outside to see if anything could be saved. What a terrifying sight met our eyes. The river was no more than 30 feet from our tent and rising visibly. Both the car and motent had been washed along about 100 yards and were luckily caught up in some low bushes by the palm trees. As we stood there watching, the motent, which was built of fibreglass, turned on its side and simply disintegrated due to the force of the water and rocks that were being carried along. I've never felt so terrified in all my life.

Once the motent had split open, its contents poured out – clothes, tins of food, binoculars, cameras and bedding. On returning to our tent, we discovered that the water had risen even higher and was by now no more than ten feet away. We hastily pulled down the tent and dragged it and our bags to the shelter of a small guardhouse a little way along the river. To our dismay it was locked and so we were forced to spend the rest of the night outside on a small covered veranda.

Johnnie and Gwen had been unable to save anything as they jumped out of the motent, and the only clothes they had were their nightwear and a pair of socks each. We shared out the blankets and sleeping bags that we had in the tent and prepared ourselves, for what turned out to be the most uncomfortable night that any of us had ever experienced. Needless to say, not one of us slept that night; we lay there wet through, with the roar of the water pounding in our ears. At long last dawn came and we cautiously left the shelter of the veranda. Fortunately the level of the water had fallen and was now only lapping around the wheels of the car. Of the caravan there only remained the chassis and a few fragments of the walls.

Our first concern was for two cameras and two pairs of binoculars that Cyril and I had left in the car. But as luck would have it, everything that had been in the car was thoroughly soaked, as well as being covered in an inch of silt. Draped amongst the bushes were many of Johnnie and Gwen's clothes, their sleeping bags and blankets. As we probed about in the sand that had been carried up by the water, we found tins of food, a tape recorder and a camera, the latter two completely ruined.

On returning to the guardhouse, we found that the two border guards were now awake, having slept through the entire night's proceedings. We explained as best we could, what had happened and they phoned through to the nearest town for assistance. Within an hour three lorries had arrived with over twenty soldiers, the chief of police and the local mayor! After several hours of pushing and pulling, the car was dragged out of the sand in which it had become deeply buried. We later learnt that the wadi had risen 13 feet above its usual level, far higher than any of the locals could remember…

For the remainder of the trip we were allowed to use one of the rooms in the guardhouse, in which we cooked and slept. Once the weather had improved we restarted netting birds, albeit with a far smaller complement of nets, as many had been lost in the flood. The number of migrant birds never really returned to their earlier levels although we continued to catch some of the more exotic European and African species such as Golden Oriole, Red-necked Nightjar, Baillon's Crake and House Bunting. Something else that I shall never forget was the need to use a Broadhurst Clarkson draw-tube telescope in the field, instead of binoculars, as mine had been ruined in the flood. Amazingly the car was eventually repaired and after three weeks at the oasis and having endured a most gruelling experience we drove north and returned home. For me a memorable introduction to Africa!

After all the excitement in Morocco, ringing at Weald Park on my return was rather an anti-climax but I still spent many hours there when I wasn't studying in London. The first week of September 1965 was a most memorable time for those lucky enough to be birding around the coasts of Norfolk and Suffolk, with one of the largest falls ever of Scandinavian drift migrants. The rarities even penetrated inland as far as Metropolitan London, for on 4th September I was lucky enough to catch a first-winter male Bluethroat at my ringing site at South Ockendon gravel pits near Hornchurch, only the third record for the London area.

Male Bluethroat ringed at South Ockendon.

Although exams and hospital residencies meant that I had far less free time in 1966, I was still able to write my first article to appear in *The Essex Bird Report* entitled The Bird Life of Weald Park 1962-1965, based on my observations and ringing there during those years. By 1967 I had qualified as a doctor and was working at Harold Wood Hospital in Essex, and once more my ringing activities picked up. I spent many happy hours ringing with my old Irish friend, Jimmy Flynn, inland at Chigwell sewage farm (where we mastered the technique of 'flicking' Swifts) and at Havering, as well as at Holliwell Point on the Essex coast, where the following year we were fortunate enough to find the first Richard's Pipit for Essex on 19th October 1968. Just three months later I had moved to Norfolk to work at the Northgate Hospital in Great Yarmouth, and thus ended my birding activities in Essex.

Jimmy Flynn admiring a Willow Warbler.

*   *   *

Chapter 3

My first visits to Norfolk

My first foray into East Anglia was a weekend visit to Havergate Island and Minsmere in Suffolk in April 1959 with David Gordon, Richard Collins and Doug Sweet, all friends from school. At the time Reg Partridge was the warden of Havergate Island and we thoroughly enjoyed the boat trip with him from Orford to Havergate and seeing for the first time the Avocets that were breeding there, as well as a host of other waders, all expertly identified by Reg. We stayed overnight at Westleton with Marjorie van Oostveen, a well-known local ornithologist who had been catering for birdwatchers for many years at the Hill Cottage guest house. She kept in her lounge a bird log, into which she invited her guests to make entries. I well remember reading about a Pomatorhine Skua (as the Pomarine Skua was known in those days) recorded by Nick Picozzi. At that stage we had not even seen Arctic or Great Skuas, let alone the rarer ones.

In 1955 Marsh Harriers nested at Minsmere for the first time, and in 1959 there were still only a handful of places in Britain where they could be found breeding. In those early days it was necessary to obtain a permit from the RSPB headquarters before visiting Minsmere, which we did, and so were able to spend a most rewarding day there on the Sunday. We were all particularly delighted to add Marsh Harrier to our life lists, albeit rather distant views, but ones that I shall never forget. We were so impressed with these two flagship RSPB reserves that we made a return visit in the autumn.

But it was not until the following year that I made my first visit to Cley in Norfolk, again with a birding friend from school, Mike Hyde, who had his own transport in the form of a battered old Ford. Despite its age and appearance, it was surprisingly reliable and I can't recall it breaking down during the week-long trip. In those days it wasn't unusual for birders to camp by the West Bank along the Beach Road at Cley, and that is exactly what we did. To save cooking over a campfire or on a primus, we mostly had fish and chips, from the excellent chippie in the village, which became one of the best places to exchange news of the latest sightings with other birders in the long queue lined up outside the serving window. It later became well known as Bryan Bland's house Flanders, so named because it was originally a slaughter house.

Bryan Bland's house in Cley, originally the old chippie. The downstairs window on the right was the serving hatch.

The week at Cley enabled us to become familiar with many of the denizens of the extensive reed beds, such as the beautiful Bearded Tit, thanks to two of the original hides approached from the East Bank, the Pool and Bittern Hides, which sadly are no longer in existence. We were also introduced to the joys of seawatching, although the lack of northerly winds, meant that it was more often than not, just that: watching the sea! In those days, shelter and back rests were provided by the concrete remains of the Cley Bird Observatory scattered along the shingle bank; formerly derelict military buildings, gun emplacements and an observation tower situated behind the beach, which had been reduced to great slabs of masonry by the 1953 east coast flood. Only four years earlier, in 1956, Collared Doves had been found nesting at Overstrand and Cromer, the first breeding records for the British Isles. So we made the short trip along the coast to Cromer, where we were delighted to find a pair sitting on a television aerial in the middle of town. Of course, unbeknown to us at the time, within a decade Collared Doves were to outnumber the then common and widespread Turtle Doves.

On our journey home back to Essex, we stopped off at Minsmere, uncertain whether or not we would be allowed to visit the Reserve, not having pre-booked any permits. Much to our delight, we were warmly welcomed by the warden Bert Axell, who always encouraged keen young birdwatchers, which of course we were at the time. He suggested that we pitch our tent on the car park by the Reserve Centre, overlooked by the specially dug sand-cliff where Sand Martins nested. To us, he seemed to be an affable, avuncular character, who couldn't have been kinder or more welcoming, although I know that he could be somewhat daunting on occasions. He subsequently became a good friend and visiting Minsmere nowadays is not quite the same. One of the other sites he suggested we visit was the Westleton rubbish tip, which we did at dusk, and had the great pleasure of watching Nightjars in flight, catching moths attracted to the beams of our car headlights.

Two more years were to pass before I made my next visit to Cley – a week's holiday with Mike Bowtell, Richard Collins and Alan Hall, in September 1962. On this occasion we stayed in Billy Bishop's green caravan that was parked in the garden behind Billy's house, Watcher's Cottage. As with Bert Axell, this was the start of a long friendship, as it was with his son, Bernard, who at the time was a young teenager. Unlike our previous visit to north Norfolk, we were blessed with northerly gales for much of the time, resulting in excellent seawatching. Without doubt this was the start of my enthusiasm for this form of birdwatching; seawatching in those days was not nearly as popular as it is today. It was also the start of my love affair with Great Skuas or Bonxies, as they are known in Scotland. During the course of one day at least 35 were recorded passing offshore, which at the time was the second highest count ever for Cley, a far cry from the totals recorded nowadays.

Mike Bowtell with a storm-driven Gannet at Cley.

Two species in particular stand out as vivid memories from that trip: Red-breasted Flycatcher and Yellow-browed Warbler. The report of a Red-breasted Flycatcher on Blakeney Point found us making the long walk along the shingle bank from Cley, and we were not disappointed for there was the little sprite feeding in the plantation on the Point before an admiring audience of at least six other birders, considered to be a real crowd in those days! Amongst them was Langley Roberts, the first warden of the Caerlaverock Reserve in Scotland. We soon fell into conversation with him and he suggested that it might well be worth our while to visit the belt of pines at Holkham, as that also acted as a magnet for fall migrants, but was checked out by very few other birdwatchers. To help us find the best areas, he drew a map in an old notebook that he had in his pocket and gave it to us. Only later did we discover that it also contained site details of some of the rare breeding birds around his Scottish home, such as Greenshank! Having had our fill of the Red-breasted Flycatcher we walked back to Cley and were soon on the road to Holkham, where we found not one but two more Red-breasted Flycatchers, and there was no-one else to show them to! They were my first records to appear in the *Norfolk Bird Report*.

An unusually large crowd admiring a Wryneck on the beach at Cley in the 1960s.

The following day we decided to once again go out to Blakeney Point and while walking through the suaeda bushes at the Long Hills with Mike Rogers, we flushed a small warbler in the company of some Goldcrests, which Mike recognised as a Yellow-browed Warbler, the first Norfolk record since 1928! Later in the day, attempts by Richard Richardson to catch it, to confirm the identification in the hand, were thwarted, as it twice flew through a mist net – the finer mesh nets were not available at that time. Nowadays it is difficult to appreciate the excitement felt by everyone who saw this Yellow-browed, in view of the vast numbers that now occur annually in the autumn.

Over the course of the next few years, I became a regular visitor to Cley, often in the company of Mike Bowtell, who was now living at Occold on the Norfolk/Suffolk border. Our visit in September 1966 is especially memorable. We were camping, as usual, by the Beach Road, and in adjoining tents were Peter Kitchener and Robin Hamilton, and we very quickly struck up a friendship that would turn out to be lifelong. We soon discovered that three of us were medical students, although Robin subsequently saw the light and changed to environmental sciences. We all had a really good birding holiday together. It was in the days before seat belts and the breathalyzer, and I can well remember the four of us driving around in my red Triumph Spitfire with the hood down, two of us in the only seats in the front and the other two perched in a well behind, sitting up on the back of the car. Robin collected skulls and he soon had a very smelly seal and porpoise skull that he had hacked off two corpses on the beach, which were slowly rotting on the grass outside his tent.

Even on the darkest nights we had no difficulty in locating our tents as we staggered back from The George, aided by the smell of rotten flesh!

But perhaps the most memorable escapade of that trip was the model of a Black-winged Stilt that we constructed and placed out on the far side of Arnold's Marsh, where it fooled many birdwatchers but not the legendary Richard Richardson. The body was made from a Heinz Baked Bean tin covered in plaster of Paris but the bright reddish-pink legs created something of a challenge. Undeterred we drove into Cromer and found just the right coloured nail varnish in the local chemist. As I handed it to the assistant to pay, Peter chirped up: "That's a perfect match with your lipstick, Moss."

Model of Black-winged Stilt at Cley in 1966.

That visit also produced my first Great Snipe, albeit one that had been shot on the marsh at Wiveton, which was brought into The George on the following evening. Two weeks earlier Ian (D.I.M.) Wallace and Bob Emmett had reported one at Salthouse, which may well have been the same bird.

Having qualified in medicine in 1967, I was now able to afford to stay at The George in Cley, rather than camping, and here we had many memorable evenings in the bar and the small room at the back (later turned into a dining room), where the birders used to congregate. At the time mine hosts were Ann and Harry Heap, whose Mynah bird did an amazing impression of the 'pips' on the radio that had us all glancing at our watches to check the time! Two permanent features of the bar seemed to be Henry Goforth, a local garage owner, and his wife Phyllis. Henry was rotund with a ruddy complexion, and was invariably to be found perched on a stool at the end of the bar looking just like Humpty Dumpty.

The George at Cley.

Aside from the birds, the highlight of many of our visits was the presence of the legendary Maury Meiklejohn, holding court in the bar. He was a great raconteur and always attracted a wide circle of birders keen to listen to his opinions and exploits in the field. Born in Hertfordshire but of Scottish parentage, he was educated at Gresham's School in Holt only a few miles from Cley, where his life-long interest in natural history was nurtured. He won an open scholarship to Oriel College, Oxford to read French and German.

Maury Meiklejohn (*anon***).**

On the Honours' Board at Greshams his name is immediately followed by that of Donald Maclean and James Klugmann, two of the infamous Cambridge spy ring, while also on the Board in the same period, 1930 – 1931, is the name of Benjamin Britten and W.H.Auden was also a contemporary – quite a collection of pupils. After graduating, Maury Meiklejohn was a lecturer at Cape Town University and served in Intelligence in the Second World War, before being appointed Professor of Italian at Glasgow University. But he never lost his love of north Norfolk and visited Cley and Blakeney several times each year. Sadly he died in 1974 at the comparatively early age of 61, sixteen years younger than I am now, and yet to me he always seemed a very wise old bird!

Honours' Board at Greshams School in Holt.

I have always been attracted to the small passerines, in particular the warblers, and three events involving *Phylloscopus* warblers remain vividly in my memory. Although I had seen the Yellow-browed Warbler on Blakeney Point in 1962, it was only thanks to brief flight views and so I was delighted on our trip to Cley in September 1967 when one that had been netted at Morston was brought along to the East Bank for birders to see in the hand. It was later released at Walsey Hills, which would have been frowned upon today. The *Norfolk Bird Report* for that year described 1967 as 'A remarkable autumn with a total of at least 9 [Yellow-browed Warblers]', showing that the species was still a great rarity throughout the 1960s.

The following year, two weekend visits to Cley with Mike Bowtell in August and October respectively resulted in us wrongly identifying two other *Phylloscopus* warblers. Firstly, one that we found in the suaeda at the Long Hills on Blakeney Point and identified as a Willow Warbler, admittedly on rather brief views, that was correctly identified later in the day by Tim Sharrock as an Arctic Warbler. We returned the next morning and obtained far better views of what was only the fourth record for Norfolk.

However, I believe that we could be excused for not correctly identifying the second bird in October, as I described in *Birds New to Norfolk*:

…On Saturday 26th October 1968 we drove up to Cley, where after a morning seawatching, we moved on to the woods at Wells and Holkham, drawn by the report of a Radde's Warbler there the previous weekend. In fact conditions were ideal for new arrivals with an overcast sky and an easterly wind. This was confirmed as we walked through the pines from Wells car park, with hundreds of Blackbirds grounded in the woods and frequent parties of Fieldfares and Redwings arriving from the north.

Between the dell and the pool, our attention was attracted by a persistent and harsh call being repeated at frequent intervals from some dense undergrowth below the silver birches. Notes taken at the time described it as a loud 'tchet', not unlike a subdued call of a Stonechat, or the churr of a Wren when it was repeated in quick succession. We were able to watch the bird, in reasonable light, down to about ten yards. [The description then followed].

As far as we were concerned, we were looking at the Radde's Warbler that had been found the previous weekend and we left the bird where we had found it, feeling very pleased with ourselves having added a new species to our life list. As we were walking back to the car, we met Keith and Enid Allsopp, and Howard Medhurst and told them about the bird, who apparently relocated it with little difficulty in view of its persistent call.

In those days the standard field guide was Peterson's *A Field Guide to the Birds of Britain and Europe*, but the edition at that time simply included the two species [Radde's and Dusky Warblers] under Accidentals at the back of the book, giving a very short description of each and certainly no pictures. I can well remember going through the descriptions in Peterson with Mike, and we both expressed some surprise that our bird showed more of the features of Dusky rather than Radde's Warbler. However, at that time it was virtually unknown for both species to be seen in the same autumn, let alone at the same location within a few days of each other.

It was only later that I learnt that our 'Radde's Warbler' had been re-identified as a Dusky Warbler, by amongst others Ron Johns. It was also joined by a second Dusky Warbler the following weekend!

It perhaps comes as little surprise that I decided to apply to work in a hospital in Norfolk, and by January 1969 I was living and working in Great Yarmouth, a move that I have never regretted.

*   *   *

Chapter 4

The golden years

I think that those of us who were fortunate enough to have been birding in Norfolk in the 1960s and 1970s would look upon them as the 'Golden Years', certainly the number of breeding birds and in particular migrants has steadily declined since then.

The real start of my love affair with Norfolk began in January 1969, when I was appointed Senior House Officer in Obstetrics & Gynaecology at Northgate Hospital in Great Yarmouth. From then on I fell in love with living and working in what was to become my adoptive county.

The author studying in the sun while on call at Northgate Hospital June 1969.

The following is a brief extract from *My Family Through Six Generations*:

Outside work, I joined the Great Yarmouth Naturalists' Society, which held its meetings in the new Yarmouth library. One of the first lectures I attended was given by Percy Trett, who was to become a good friend (although his repeated attempts to get me to join the Freemasons failed totally!). The subject of his lecture was the Yarmouth naturalist, Arthur Patterson, who was to become one of my local heroes. I also started to meet the Yarmouth birders, including Peter Allard, who introduced me to the best birding localities in the area, such as Yarmouth Cemetery and the extensive dunes at Winterton. Another local birder, Andrew Grieve, was still living at home with his parents at Caister-on-Sea, although he subsequently moved to the RSPB reserve at Blacktoft Sands in Yorkshire, where he worked as the longest-ever serving RSPB warden. By now Mike Bowtell was living near Diss in Suffolk, while fellow medic and birding friend, Peter Kitchener, was working at the Norfolk & Norwich Hospital. We spent many enjoyable and successful days out together, especially during the autumn.

One of the first birds that I saw in Great Yarmouth was a Collared Dove on a nest in the grounds of Northgate Hospital in mid-January, bringing back happy memories of my first at Cromer nine years earlier, although of course, by 1969 they had spread to most parts of Britain & Ireland. I thoroughly enjoyed working and living in Yarmouth in the winter, the first occasion that I had ever lived by the coast with all its birding attractions such as wintering gulls and wildfowl. Nearby, Buckenham Marshes hosted a regular flock of the only wintering Taiga Bean Geese in England, although I never did catch up with a Lesser White-fronted Goose that occasionally joined them, and I still have yet to see a genuinely wild one.

On 21st June I was invited to join Peter Allard on a trip to Cantley to see a singing Great Reed Warbler that had been found by John Bruhn at one of his ringing sites three days earlier. It was here that I first met the doyen of Norfolk's birding fraternity, Michael Seago. The following day I made the first of many ringing visits over the course of the next couple of years to Winterton dunes, often in the company of Peter Allard, Terry Boulton or Andrew Grieve, all of whom lived in the Yarmouth area. The dune slacks, in which grew a few stunted bushes, proved to be the most rewarding areas for mist netting migrants and we ringed several Wrynecks, as well as a brood of Red-backed Shrikes, the nest being only four feet from the ground in a small rhododendron bush. How things have changed. One day in particular stands out in my memory, 20th September 1969, following a classic fall of Scandinavian migrants around the coast of Norfolk associated with north-easterly winds, overnight rain and a sea mist. Conservative estimates included 5+ Wrynecks, 30 Whinchats, 50 Common Redstarts and a Tawny Pipit. While Yarmouth Cemetery held 40 Common Redstarts, 15 Pied Flycatchers, and a single Icterine Warbler and Red-breasted Flycatcher. It was the first time that I had experienced one of these famous east coast autumn falls, which surely must rate as one of the most exciting birding experiences.

The author watching a Wryneck at Winterton with from left to right Andrew Grieve, Terry Boulton, Mike Bowtell & Peter Kitchener on 20th Sept 1969 (*Peter Allard*).

Not surprisingly I opted to stay on at Northgate Hospital for a second six-month appointment, this time as a Senior House Officer in Medicine, a decision that was justified when a Cream-coloured Courser was found at Blakeney in mid-October. Fortunately it remained in the Morston area until my next day off, where I was delighted to see it in the same field as a Hoopoe! Although it disappeared after about ten days, amazingly it was re-found just north of Yarmouth at Caister-on-Sea, where I was able to watch it once again. The full story was delightfully told by Peter Allard in the *Norfolk Bird & Mammal Report 1969*:

> Whilst searching for a Richard's Pipit in a partly harvested sugar beet field at Blakeney on 18th October, a visiting ornithologist spotted a Cream-coloured Courser arriving from the direction of the saltings. Within a very short time a small army of bird-watchers had seen this stranger and by the weekend coaches were arriving from the Midlands and the London area.
>
> It seemed quite content in its surroundings, finding an abundance of food. Against the light sandy soil it was very inconspicuous, running at speed in an almost endless series of dashes. Occasionally it concealed itself in small depressions in the ground. Curiously the very first Norfolk record was at nearby Morston 122 years ago. The courser remained in this area until mid-day on 29th – a day of strong north-westerly winds. That afternoon in East Norfolk, a tractor driver harvesting beet at Ormesby East End noticed an unusual bird arriving from the north at 1530 hours. This was soon identified as a Cream-coloured Courser and, as in North Norfolk, the news quickly spread. Within days this desert stranger was attracting observers from as far away as Devon, Gloucestershire and Yorkshire. It seems fairly certain that these records relate to the one bird…
>
> The Ormesby courser favoured two partly harvested sugar-beet fields close to the sea; one morning it appeared in a farmyard only to be disturbed by an over-keen photographer. As the days passed, it became more tame despite constant disturbance. By 9th November it could be approached to within two feet following the arrival of much colder weather. During this period it was fed with maggots, which it took readily and was last seen alive on the 15th. On 20th November it was found dead in the field where it was first seen at Ormesby East End. The skin is preserved in Norwich Castle Museum.

Cream-coloured Courser by R.A.Richardson.

This constituted only the fourth record for Norfolk and none has been reported in the county since. Despite the fact that it occurred over 50 years ago, some very interesting parallels are apparent in Peter Allard's account. Although it was before the advent of telephone birdlines, pagers, mobile phones, apps, birding websites and other forms of social media, the news was still spread extremely quickly by word of mouth, land lines and birding grapevines, and as a result 'twitchers' (although this term had not been invented by then) were soon at the scene from all over Britain. But worryingly, even in those days bird photographers were not content to remain at a sensible distance, although of course, telephoto lenses were far less effective than they are nowadays. There is also an interesting parallel with the Isabelline Wheatear at Cley in late autumn 2019, whose life was almost certainly extended by the provision of mealworms.

Just two weeks later, on 2nd November 1969, I once more made the journey from Yarmouth to the north Norfolk coast, this time to see a dowitcher at Cley, as I recounted in a short article in the autumn 2017 *Cley Bird Club Newsletter*:

> A dowitcher, of undetermined species, had earlier been reported from the pool at Weybourne Hope on October 30th, and was then re-located on the North Scrape by Owen Laugharne on November 2nd. So it was to the North Hide that I made my way from the beach car park as soon as I arrived. Only a handful of other birders were present in the hide, but we were probably considered a 'crowd' in those days! Amongst those present were Keith and Enid Allsopp (aka Natterjack). Unfortunately the dowitcher was on the far side of the pool on North Scrape, and even with the latest Hertel & Reuss telescopes its specific identification could not be ascertained. However, Enid Allsopp came to the rescue by playing first of all a tape recording of Short-billed Dowitcher, which elicited no response whatsoever and then the flight call of a Long-billed Dowitcher. The effect was amazing with the bird immediately taking off, calling in response and flying towards the North Hide – problem solved! From the NBR Record Card, I see that the bird was also seen by Ian (D.I.M.) Wallace on November 4th, the last date on which it was recorded, but it may well be that we are the only two observers still alive who were lucky enough to see this 'first' for the Cley Reserve.

On 1st March 1970 I started a six-month appointment in Paediatrics at St Peter's Hospital, Chertsey in Surrey, but pressure of work meant that I had little time for birding. I couldn't wait to get back to Norfolk and was lucky enough to be offered a post as Medical Registrar at the Norfolk & Norwich Hospital, where my old friend Peter Kitchener was also working. Following my marriage to Fran in September, we initially lived in married accommodation on St Stephens Road, opposite the old Norfolk & Norwich Hospital, before buying a bungalow at Little Plumstead, where we were to live for the next year. At last I was to live permanently in my adoptive county of Norfolk and once more started to ring birds on a regular basis, an interest that was to continue for the next 45 years.

Although I ringed over 500 birds in the garden of Willows End, our bungalow at Little Plumstead, the main focus of my ringing was the many pairs of Swallows that were nesting on the farms in the area. During the two summers of 1971 and 1972

I ringed over 450 Swallow nestlings, one of which provided me with my first published 'Note' in *British Birds*:

Congenital bill deformity in nestling Swallow On 19th May 1971, while ringing a brood of five Swallows *Hirundo rustica* at Little Plumstead, Norfolk, I noticed that one of the nestlings had a congenital deformity of the bill. On closer examination it was apparent that the upper mandible, palate and tongue were all affected. The shape of the bird's bill is illustrated in fig. 1; the palate was centrally cleft and the tongue bifid. Despite this handicap the bird later flew successfully along with the rest of the brood. During the following four months a total of 301 nestling Swallows were ringed and closely examined, and no other external congenital abnormalities were detected.

In Dr D. E. Pomeroy's paper 'Birds with abnormal bills' (*Brit. Birds*, 55: 49-72) no similar deformity was described and indeed the Swallow was not mentioned as a species in which a bill deformity of any nature had been recorded, which seems surprising in view of the large numbers ringed annually.

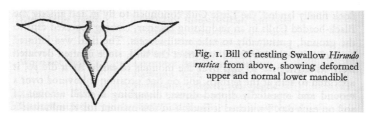

Fig. 1. Bill of nestling Swallow *Hirundo rustica* from above, showing deformed upper and normal lower mandible

Dr Pomeroy commented: 'Congenital abnormalities of the bill are not often recorded in wild birds… One of the few records involving hirundines is, however, somewhat similar: it concerns an African Cliff Swallow *H. spilodera* with "degenerate lower mandible overlapped by the maxilla.'

As with the majority of small passerines the recovery rate for the Swallows was extremely low, and only two of the nestlings were subsequently recovered: one locally in Little Plumstead, but the other more excitingly was controlled (retrapped by another ringer) in South Africa eight months after being ringed. In fact this very bird was the reason that I entitled an article in the March 2010 *Cley Bird Club Newsletter*, "A Tale of Two Swallows" that described a birding holiday in South Africa in January of that year and concluded with:

So why did I call this article 'A Tale of Two Swallows'? Well, back in the 1970s when I lived in Norwich, I ringed a large number of Swallow nestlings, one of which was controlled at Firgrove in Cape Province, South Africa. Imagine my surprise when I discovered that Brian Van der Walt, who was in the hide [with us] at the Langebaan Lagoon, was one of the team that had controlled my Swallow at Firgrove back in 1973. But the co-incidence didn't stop there. One of the three birders from Australia, Dave Henderson, who was also in the hide, turned out to be a fellow ringer from Essex, and we had also exchanged ringed Swallows back in 1965! The world is truly a small place.

In April 1972, Fran, Chris (our one-month old son) and I moved to Sheringham, where I have lived for the last 48 years and where I hope to see out my days. I have absolutely no wish to move away from what I now consider to be my spiritual home, surrounded by the beautiful Norfolk countryside, even if spreading urban development is encroaching on it at a worryingly rapid pace.

Sheringham from Beeston Hill in 2014.

*   *   *

Chapter 5

Dead Man's Wood

Anyone looking at the Ordnance Survey map covering the north-east Norfolk coast will see a small 14-acre wood between Sheringham and Weybourne, officially in the Civil Parish of Upper Sheringham, called Dead Man's Hill. The origin of its name is debateable. It is situated 400 yards inland from the coast, opposite the deeper water at Spalla Gap, where there is a natural hollow between the low sandy cliffs. However, I like to believe that it was the traditional burial site for smugglers and pirates, who had died and whose bodies were carried up from their ships and boats anchored off Spalla Gap, to be buried on the higher ground at Dead Man's Hill. Whatever the origin of the name, it is now better known as Dead Man's Wood, and as from 1987 is included in the National Trust's Sheringham Park, having previously been part of the Upcher Estate. Its position makes it ideal for attracting migrating birds in both spring and autumn.

Back in 1972, when I moved to Sheringham, it was an impenetrable mature Scots pine wood with sea buckthorn, elderberry and bramble bushes along the northern side and a narrow line of scrub running from the north-west corner down to Spalla Gap, which acted as a corridor for birds arriving from the north and so channelled them up to the wood. A few hundred yards to the east of the wood, a sea buckthorn hedge ran north to south, from the cliff-top path to the railway line. This too acted as a magnet for newly arrived migrants, and it was along this 60-foot wide hedge that I first started to deploy my mist nets, in the autumn of 1972. In fact it was difficult to know exactly where to concentrate my efforts, as far as ringing was concerned, as there were virtually no other active ringers in this part of the county.

My free time, as the junior partner in a three-man general medical practice, was severely limited. Did I concentrate on ringing garden birds or nestlings in the nest boxes at Beeston Hall School (where the pairs of nesting Tree Sparrows easily outnumbered the tits)? By late July I was also being tempted by the roost of hirundines and wagtails in the reed bed at Weybourne Hope, as well as the migrants in the sea buckthorn hedge near Dead Man's Wood, where my efforts were rewarded with a Barred Warbler netted in September, along with over 50 Tree Sparrows, a species that nowadays I'm lucky to see once a year! Unfortunately the sea buckthorns were grubbed up, as the local farmer considered they were harbouring a healthy, or rather unhealthy, population of rabbits.

But as it turned out, my mind was made up for me by an exceptional influx of redpolls. By chance, from early October I had started ringing in the woods behind Wiveton Hall by kind permission of the father of Desmond MacCarthy, star of the BBC's television series 'Normal for Norfolk'. Between 7th October and 19th December over 200 redpolls were ringed, including no fewer than 96 Mealy and three Arctic Redpolls. I took one of the Arctics to Cley to show Richard Richardson, when he was living in the High Street. At the time only five had ever been ringed in Britain, and they were considered to be very rare birds, so Richard was extremely pleased to see one in the hand.

However, it was not until 4th August 1974 that I started to ring in Dead Man's Wood, thanks to the endeavours of the senior partner in my practice, Dr Harry

Cowper-Johnson, who was part of the syndicate that shot in Dead Man's Wood and over the surrounding fields. Through him, I was given permission to set up a ringing station in the wood, provided we did not net on the days that the shoots took place.

Despite the prevailing westerly winds during most of the autumn of 1974, no fewer than 690 birds of 39 species were ringed. Of these almost 600 were netted in August and September alone, thus demonstrating the great potential of the wood as a ringing site, while observations indicated its value as a migration watch point. The only easterly winds of the autumn occurred over the last weekend in August (which strangely enough almost always produces favourable winds) and resulted in a small fall of Whinchats, Pied Flycatchers and Willow Warblers, as well as a Wood Warbler, a species rarely recorded on autumn migration in Norfolk. At the start, facilities for ringing and processing the birds were very basic, as is shown in the photo below, where most of the table appears to be occupied by cups and cans of beer!

David Sadler & Billy Little ringing at Dead Man's Wood in August 1974.

But things began to change in 1975, as was described in the Introduction to the *Dead Man's Wood Report* for that year:

> Although one visit was made to the wood in February, regular observations were not started until the end of March. At this time a hut was erected on the northern edge of the wood, which has made an ideal ringing laboratory and hide. Six polythene-lined pools were constructed near some of the net sites and these undoubtedly attracted many birds to the nets. In addition, ten closed and two open-fronted nest boxes were put up.

Ringing hut in 1976.

Incidentally, the original ringing hut is still being used 45 years later (although far less regular ringing is now undertaken). As a BTO 'A' ringer, I was able to take on some trainees and within a year or so two keen local birders, David Sadler and Kevin Shepherd, had both obtained sufficient experience to be awarded their 'C' ringing permits. By the end of the following year, Pete Smith had also joined us and had been trained up as a 'C' ringer, thus enabling far better coverage, particularly during the spring and autumn, as both he and David Sadler were school masters and thus available during the school holidays. Again the Introduction to the *Sheringham Ringing Report 1976* provides a flavour of the progress that had been made at the wood, in just two years:

> 1976 was a year that will long be remembered by the ringers operating in Dead Man's Wood. During the year, 3529 birds of 64 species were ringed, while 174 species were recorded in the area. The excellent total was, without doubt, due to the very full coverage maintained throughout the spring and autumn. Except for one day, the wood was visited daily between March 27th and May 20th; and between July 16th and September 2nd, ringing was undertaken on every day except two.
>
> The spring was notable for the passage of Cardueline finches, especially redpolls and Goldfinches... Rarities and semi-rarities recorded during the year included Leach's Petrel, Iceland, Mediterranean and Sabine's Gulls, Wryneck, Barred and Pallas's Warblers, and Arctic Redpoll.

I well remember phoning Chris Mead at the Ringing Office in Beech Grove, to tell him that we had ringed over 450 Goldfinches, and he thought that I was talking about the previous autumn, as this number ringed in the spring at a single site was unprecedented. He persuaded me to write it up and an article about the movement of Cardueline finches appeared in the *Sheringham Ringing Report 1976*, excerpts from which follow:

> During spring 1976, a large number of Cardueline finches was trapped in Dead Man's Wood, Sheringham. Between March 6th and May 25th, 473 Goldfinches, 107 Siskins, 322 Lesser, 51 Mealy and 2 Arctic Redpolls were ringed... [The vast majority] were caught at mist net sites at which small polythene-lined pools had been constructed, to which the birds frequently dropped to drink and bathe. While for a considerable part of the day, the birds remained in the pines, feeding on the cones, singing and preening.
>
> Lesser Redpolls and Siskins were the predominant species in March, with the latter peaking in the last third of the month. While Lesser Redpoll numbers remained fairly constant during April and May, Mealy Redpolls arrived at the end of March, peaked in the first half of April and had virtually disappeared by the end of the month. Goldfinches, however, first appeared in any numbers in the last third of April, with a peak in the first third of May, and very few after the 18th.
>
> Only Goldfinches were noted on visible migration in any numbers, and even then not in April. Between May 1st and June 13th,

when weather conditions were suitable (fine, warm days with a gentle south-westerly wind) a regular westerly movement was logged, with parties of up to 30 birds flying resolutely west over the beach or cliffs, at a height of about 20 feet. Peak counts were made on May 1st (600), 8th (200) and 11th (520) with the majority passing between dawn and 1000hrs.

An even more impressive day count was made at Dead Man's Wood on 26th April 1977 when 1,700 flew west, a number that is unlikely to be exceeded as I explained in the species text for Goldfinch in *The Norfolk Bird Atlas*:

> Up to at least the 1980s, more than 80% of British Goldfinches moved south in autumn to winter in Belgium, France and Spain, a partial migration that involved mainly female and first-winter birds. As breeding populations have risen over recent years, it appears that far fewer birds may now be undertaking this southerly movement in autumn. A rise in numbers wintering in Norfolk is most evident in gardens, where Goldfinches have become regular visitors to feeding stations, being particularly attracted to niger seeds and sunflower hearts. These are both products only recently on the bird food market and perhaps instrumental in enabling Goldfinches to overwinter in such numbers.

Fulmar ringing team at Dead Man's Wood in 1984, in back row Dave Horsley, Dave Appleton, David Sadler, Clive Slater, Pete Smith and kneeling Chris Taylor and Chris Adams.

It was also in the mid-1970s that we started to ring the adult and nestling Fulmars on the cliffs between Sheringham and Weybourne, and by the end of 1984 a total of 154 had been ringed. Fulmars were first noted prospecting the cliffs at Weybourne in 1940, but it was not until 1947, encouraged by artificial ledges cut out by the well-known Norfolk ornithologist Dick Bagnall-Oakeley and his pupils at Gresham's School, that successful breeding was first proved in Norfolk, when five pairs were present. By co-incidence, one of the schoolboys who helped cut out these ledges was David Sadler, and it was he that was often lowered on a rope to the breeding ledges when the Fulmar nestlings were ringed in the 1970s. This was before Health & Safety legislation, and our antics would certainly have been frowned upon today. Often the rope around the waist of the ringer descending to the ledges was simply held at the top by two other members of the team, although in later years, we did tie it around a sturdy post hammered into the ground.

Kevin Shepherd & Clive McKay preparing to be lowered to a ledge in 1981.

We all took it in turns to be lowered down to the ledge, where we were invariably covered in partly digested, fowl-smelling fish that was regurgitated by the young Fulmar. In fact the smell was so revolting that my wife insisted that my 'Fulmar ringing clothes' were not allowed into the house, and had to be stored in the garden shed.

Dave Horsley and Pete Smith with a Fulmar nestling in 1984.

In addition to the nestlings we were also ringing some of the adults, at least those that were on ledges near enough to the top to be caught in a long-handled landing net. On this occasion the operative dangled over the edge of the cliff with his assistant holding on to his ankles! Amazingly, we had no accidents. By 1984, 50-60 pairs of Fulmars nested on the cliffs between Weybourne and Cromer and sufficient numbers had been ringed and recovered to warrant an article in the *Norfolk Bird & Mammal Report 1984*, entitled Origins and Movements of Norfolk Fulmars, some extracts from which follow:

Up to the end of 1984, a total of 21 Fulmars ringed outside the county had been found in Norfolk. The great majority were ringed at Scottish colonies (Shetlands 8, Orkneys 4 and the Scottish mainland 5), with singles from the Farnes, Iceland, Norway and the North Sea…[These included] an adult trapped on a ledge at Sheringham in March 1984, which had been ringed as a nestling on the Farne Islands.

In common with many species of seabird, Fulmars take several years to reach sexual maturity, and are usually 6-12 years old before first attempting to breed. Only two Norfolk-ringed nestlings have been found again in Norfolk in subsequent years. Both were found dead on the beach in July below breeding colonies, not far from their natal ledges, seven and eight years respectively after hatching. Despite ringing over 100 nestlings at Sheringham, none has yet been caught again back on a breeding ledge. Thus there is only circumstantial evidence to suggest that the birds are returning to breed at or near their natal colonies.

By 1978, Kevin Shepherd had been awarded his 'A' ringing permit and could thus take over the running of the ringing at Dead Man's Wood, although by 1980 he was spending most of the year at University and so I returned as the official 'A' ringer at the wood for a couple of years. This was a decision that I certainly did not regret in October 1982, as I described in an article in the series "Memorable Days" in the *Norfolk Bird Club Bulletin* in February 2002:

Until I retired, September and October were always frustrating months for me. I was invariably on call, whenever a good east wind was blowing, and all I could do on such occasions was to stay at home and dream about the birds I knew I was missing. Although my annual birding holiday in October was often characterised by westerly winds, I felt sure that one year my luck would change.

Saturday 9th October 1982 was the start of my annual week's birding, and as I had come to expect, the wind was not blowing from an easterly quarter. In fact it was north-north-west force six, gusting up to gale force eight. A visit to Dead Man's Wood in the morning was not very promising and the only bird of note was a single Pied Flycatcher. I can't remember whether it was news from the local grapevine or just a visit on the off chance, but the afternoon found me in Wells woods, where there was a great deal of activity both amongst the birds and the birders. A large arrival of Goldcrests had ensured that every small passerine was being carefully checked as birds flitted from branch to branch in the pines and silver birches.

I was soon on to a gem of a Pallas's Warbler feeding unconcerned, only a few yards away, in the trees on the north side of the car park, to be followed within half-an-hour by a second in the Dell. As I commented in my notebook: '…double yellow wing-bars, yellow supercilium, yellow central crown stripe and yellow rump – what more can you want in a bird!' But the bird that was causing most excitement and interest was a Radde's Warbler, only the eighth county record and, if only I could see it, a lifer for me. Eventually my patience was rewarded, as it appeared, albeit rather briefly, skulking low down in a tangle of brambles. By now it was late afternoon, and any thoughts of returning to Dead Man's that day were clearly impractical.

After a rather fitful night's sleep, during which I awoke every half-an-hour, I arrived at Dead Man's just before dawn. By now the wind had dropped to force 2-3, but was still coming from the north-west. As I went around the wood putting up my nets, it was only too apparent that a good-sized 'fall' had occurred since my visit the previous day. Robins were ticking from every available piece of cover, Blackcaps were scolding from the elderberry bushes and the thin 'tsee-tsee-tsee' of Goldcrests was audible throughout the canopy of the pines. Flighty Song Thrushes were constantly on the move in the wood and my first Fieldfares of the autumn flew off noisily inland.

Each round of the nets produced new birds to ring, the most numerous being Goldcrests with a sprinkling of Robins and *Sylvia* warblers. The first bird of note in the hand was a Chiffchaff of the eastern race *tristis*, followed in the middle of the morning by a Yellow-browed Warbler, surprisingly the first record for Dead Man's Wood. Being alone, I was kept so busy all morning, constantly checking the nets, and extracting and ringing birds, that I had little opportunity to look around for new arrivals. But the best was yet to come.

The constant stream of Goldcrests finding their way into the nets showed no signs of abating and even by early afternoon, one particular net site in the centre of the wood was still catching well. But I was somewhat taken aback to discover a rather dull brown, non-descript, *Phylloscopus* warbler, with a long, broad pale buff supercilium sharing the net with 15 Goldcrests. A detailed examination of the bird in the ringing hut confirmed my initial suspicions that this was indeed a Dusky Warbler, not only another new bird for Dead Man's, but only the second ever to be ringed in Norfolk! Of course, on being released it immediately disappeared into deep cover, but not before giving its characteristic Lesser Whitethroat-like call. Naturally I returned home elated, not least because the day's ringing total was in excess of 100. In the two days I had seen Yellow-browed, Pallas's, Radde's and Dusky Warblers!

Dusky Warbler at Dead Man's Wood on 9th October 1982.

After yet another restless night, dawn once again found me in Dead Man's, where my mist nets were soon erected. Almost the first bird trapped was the ringed Dusky Warbler, but unfortunately again it was not seen in the field. The Yellow-browed, however, did perform well, calling constantly from the sallows, where it actively fed in the open for most of the day.

The wind by now had veered to north-north-east force 2-3, and the overcast skies once again produced ideal conditions for netting. A Belgian-ringed Blackcap that appeared in one of the nets was our first foreign control for this species, the bird having been ringed in Flanders two weeks earlier. Surely that would be the highlight of the day, but no it wasn't to be. The second BB rarity in as many days, turned up in one of the nets along the northern edge of the wood: a Little Bunting, another new species for Dead Man's and the first to be ringed in the county. The Wryneck that I found in the afternoon, feeding along the railway line behind the wood, was almost an anticlimax!

For me, at least, such an exciting two days was never to be repeated at my ringing site in Dead Man's Wood.

After graduating and moving back to Sheringham in the mid to late 1980s, Kevin Shepherd joined David Sadler, who by now held an 'A' ringing permit and between them they jointly managed the ringing site well into the new millennium. They were joined over the next few years by several other local birders, including Steve Votier, Tim Wright, Mike Young-Powell, Paul Lee, Andy Benson and Dave Appleton, some of whom also trained as ringers, as well as many other well-known names. In 1993, the surge of interest and enthusiasm for recording visible migration at the site, as well as ringing birds, resulted in renaming it the Sheringham Bird Observatory. Five species recorded in the vicinity of Dead Man's Wood have constituted the first county records: Paddyfield and Lanceolated Warblers, Alpine Accentor, Blyth's Pipit and as recently as 2019 Upland Sandpiper. Although far less ringing is currently carried out at Dead Man's, regular observations there still make a valuable contribution to our understanding of migration along the north Norfolk coast.

*   *   *

Chapter 6

Cley – the birdwatchers' Mecca

Following the death of Mr A.W.Cozens-Hardy of Cley Hall, part of his estate, a block of 435 acres of grazing marsh between the coast road and the beach, was put up for auction in March 1926. Following a tidal surge five years earlier a large part of the area had started to revert to reedbeds with surrounding flooded meadows, which in turn attracted a wide variety of breeding waders, including a pair of Ruffs that nested and laid four eggs in 1922. Living in Norwich at this time was a physician, Dr Sydney Long, who worked at the Norfolk & Norwich and Jenny Lind Hospitals, but was also a very keen naturalist and conservationist. On learning about the sale of the marshes at Cley, he persuaded a friend to contribute £4,000 towards the likely auction price and Dr Long's bid of £5,160 was successful in purchasing both the marsh and a building plot on the other side of the coast road, where Watcher's Cottage now stands.

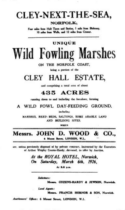

CLEY-NEXT-THE-SEA,
NORFOLK,

Four miles from Holt Town and Station, 1 mile from Blakeney, 10 miles from Wells, and 12 miles from Cromer.

UNIQUE
Wild Fowling Marshes
ON THE NORFOLK COAST,

being a portion of the
CLEY HALL ESTATE,

and comprising a total area of about
435 ACRES

running down to and including the foreshore, forming
A WILD FOWL DAY-FEEDING GROUND,
including
MARSHES, REED-BEDS, SALTINGS, SOME ARABLE LAND
AND BUILDING SITES,
WHICH

Messrs. JOHN D. WOOD & CO.,
6 Mount Street, LONDON, W.1,

are, unless previously disposed of by private contract, instructed by the Executors of Arthur Wrigley Cozens-Hardy, deceased, to offer by Auction.

At the ROYAL HOTEL, Norwich,
On Saturday, March 6th, 1926,
At 3.0 p.m.

Solicitors:
Messrs. COZENS-HARDY & JEWSON, Norwich.
Land Agents:
Messrs. FRANCIS HORNOR & SON, Norwich.

Auctioneers' Offices: 6 Mount Street, LONDON, W.1.

Notice re Sale of Cley Marshes in 1926.

A week later at a celebratory lunch party at the George Hotel, Cley Sydney Long presented his ideas about the formation of an organisation to own and manage the newly-acquired Cley marshes. Eight months later the Norfolk Naturalists Trust was formally incorporated and Cley Marsh became its first reserve. Since then the Cley area has attracted not only a most impressive number of breeding and wintering species, as well as vagrant birds from all over the world, but also thousands of birdwatchers, many of whom have made the decision to move to Cley and make it their permanent home. It is about these human residents and visitors that this chapter is mainly concerned.

One of the first things that Sydney Long did after the formation of the Norfolk Naturalists Trust was to appoint Bob Bishop, an old fisherman and wildfowler, as the first warden or 'Watcher' of the Cley Marshes Reserve. Then 11 years later in 1937, Bob Bishop's grandson, Billy Bishop, was appointed as the new Warden. In only his first year, Billy was delighted to find a Bittern's nest at Cley, within 200 yards of his house. The nest contained four eggs and Sydney Long drove straight up to Cley to see the nest for himself, as the species had never before been recorded as breeding at

Cley. In 1940 Billy joined the Navy, to return as Warden after the war. Despite being a reserve, the marshes were still let out during the winter for duck shooting, in fact up to the mid-1960s, which along with selling cut reeds for thatching and letting out the grazing on the marshes, helped to finance the upkeep of the area. Billy believed that coypu were largely responsible for the subsequent decline of Bitterns and possibly Marsh Harriers in the reedbeds, and between 1947 and 1978 over 6,000 coypu were shot. However, it wasn't only coypu that were being shot and it wasn't until 1955, after the 1954 Protection of Birds Act had been passed, that shooting was finally stopped from the East Bank.

Billy Bishop enjoying a hot toddy before a coypu shoot (*anon*).

When I first used to come to Cley back in the early 1960s, my visits were never complete unless I had seen Billy Bishop, Richard Richardson and if I was particularly fortunate, Dick Bagnall-Oakeley. Of all three, Billy was generally the easiest to locate, either at home in Watcher's Cottage or in 'Billy's hut', which was situated on slightly elevated land to the east, between the houses on the coast road and Snipes' Marsh. Here it was possible to obtain permits to visit the hides, and from here Billy was able to keep a watchful eye on his Reserve. It was from here that Billy initially saw Norfolk's first Black-winged Pratincole, as I described in *Guardian Spirit of the East Bank*, which also included an extract from Richard Richardson's personal diary of his sightings at Cley in 1966:

"3rd July: WFB spotted a strange bird from the roadside hide which turned out to be a beautiful Black-winged Pratincole. Everyone here watched it for the whole day from 0930hrs GMT. It spent much of its time on the 'Bath Marsh' (about 400 yards from the Coast Road), either just sitting and preening or running swiftly about to snap at flies on the grass. Sometimes it flew round above the marsh like a large wader swerving from side to side and doubling back with a graceful agile flight. Often it climbed steeply into the air like a Black Tern to take a high-flying insect and it was frequently chased by Lapwings, Black-headed Gulls and once a Common Tern. The black wing-linings were clearly visible as it banked close by in brilliant sunshine and the absence of white on the tips of the secondaries confirmed the identification. The upper parts were rich brown and the breast was paler than I'd expected. The forked tail and white rump were very noticeable. After each quick run along the ground it wagged its hind-parts up and down. A new bird for Norfolk and for everyone who saw it."

The story of the discovery of this bird and its eventual identification is possibly apocryphal but is nevertheless worth repeating. When initially spotted by Billy Bishop it was flying in front of the roadside hide, from where the reserve permits were sold. He identified it as a swift from its outline and the fact that it was hawking for insects; it then landed on the dry marsh and he thought it was a tern; finally it started to run around whereupon he immediately realised it was actually a pratincole!

Naturally Richard produced a delightful montage in watercolours of the pratincole, which he gave to Billy as a gift. This was one of several paintings that Richard gave to Billy, usually of birds that Billy had found on the Reserve. After Billy died it was bequeathed to his grandson, Darren, from whom the author purchased it in 2010. Ironically, the money was used to buy a new shot gun!

Black-winged Pratincole at Cley in 1966.

It would be very easy to devote a whole chapter to Richard Richardson, one of my lifetime heroes, but to give a flavour of his remarkable life, his artistic skills and expertise in the field, as well as his influence on a generation of birders in the 1950s, 60s and 70s, I am simply going to present some extracts from four of my *Eastern Daily Press* In the Countryside columns, written between 2000 and 2002:

Born at Blackheath in south London in 1922, Richard moved to Norfolk in 1940, when he joined The Royal Norfolk Regiment. He was billeted at Aylsham until embarkation for the Far East in 1943. He served with his regiment in India, Ceylon and Singapore, before returning to England after the war. In 1949 he moved to Cley-next-the-Sea, where he lived for the rest of his life, and in the same year he established the Cley Bird Observatory, serving as its only warden until it closed in 1963…

… As a teenager, my visits to Cley were incomplete unless I had met Richard, usually at the end of the East Bank overlooking Arnold's Marsh, in his leather jacket and beret, and often accompanied by his two small terriers. In common with many other young birdwatchers of the time, he became my mentor for many years. However, his talents were not confined to field observations and his accurate portrayal of birds in watercolours. He was also a first-class writer producing delightful written descriptions of birding scenes.

Unfortunately, following his death, most of his personal bird diaries went missing, but recently the original folder containing his first draft of a book he was planning to write, entitled "Birds of Cley", has come to light. Although less than 20 species' accounts have been completed, each one is a tribute to Richard's skill as an author. Under Bluethroats on Blakeney Point he writes "[Observers] have made pilgrimages there, hoping to catch a glimpse of this spry and elusive little bird with the black and chestnut tail. More often than not, the tail is all they do see as the bird reluctantly breaks cover beneath their feet and with low, fast flight and an adroit twist drops suddenly back into the *Suaeda*. If one is patient, however, and waits quietly by the dunes, the hungry Bluethroat will emerge into the daylight from its secret, shell-paved corridors under the tangled stems and hop like a robin on the sand, nervously flicking its tail, always ready to scuttle back into concealment on its spindly legs"…

…As a self-taught artist, Richard had been perfecting his skills at bird illustration since his teenage years. His prodigious talent was first recognised by the author and naturalist Richard Fitter in the late 1940s. Together they worked on the highly successful *Pocket Guide to British Birds* and *Pocket Guide to Nests and Eggs*, published by Collins in the 1950s. His illustrations subsequently appeared in over 20 books, as well as many annual bird reports… His watercolours still adorn the walls of many birdwatchers who knew him. He rarely sketched in the field, the vast majority of his work being produced at home, on the kitchen table, from images in his mind's eye.

Richard Richardson painting at Cley in 1954 (*anon*).

But perhaps his greatest gift, was his ability to communicate with birdwatchers of any age, beginners or experts alike. He would invariably be found on the East Bank at Cley, along with his two Norfolk terriers, surrounded by a group of admirers, keen to learn from this unassuming expert. His skill as a field ornithologist is legendary and he is still remembered as a treasured friend by many, despite dying in 1977.

The third of my non-avian targets on my visits to Cley in the 1960s was Dick Bagnall-Oakeley about whom I wrote in *Rare and Scarce Birds in North-east Norfolk*:

Dick Bagnall-Oakeley, was born in Norwich in 1908. His father, the Rev. Kemeys Bagnall-Oakeley, was Vicar of Hemsby, and it was here that Dick was initially educated at Hemsby council school. Here he mixed with the local children and quickly picked up the authentic Norfolk dialect, as a result of which he was able to drop into 'Broad Norfolk' at any time. He was subsequently educated at Gresham's School in Holt, becoming School Captain in his final year, and left in 1927. In the following year he went up to Clare College, Cambridge, where he graduated with a First in Geography. After a year at home, he went to Norwich Art School before returning as a teacher to

41

Gresham's School. As well as being an inspirational teacher to generations of schoolboys, Dick was renowned for his exceptional eyesight and of the many tales about this attribute, the one relating to his medical prior to being accepted as an officer in the School O.T.C. is delightfully described by Logie Bruce Lockhart in his booklet *Dick Bagnall-Oakeley - A Tribute to a Norfolk Naturalist*:

"Mr H. Barney reminded us that the barracks where the medical was held are on the top of a hill overlooking the [Norwich] Cathedral. The M.O.'s room was several storeys high. The sight test began. On being asked to read the bottom line of the test card, Dick replied 'Printed by De la Rue & Co'. This was printed microscopically at the left hand of the bottom of the sheet and was not meant to be part of the test. The M.O. was so surprised that he asked Dick for more examples of his power of sight. Dick told him that he habitually read a newspaper on the floor from a standing position. In disbelief the M.O. pointed to the weathercock at the top of the distant Cathedral and asked whether Dick could describe any details. Having taken pictures of the weathercock with his telescopic lens Dick knew all about it. His description was confirmed by the M.O. through binoculars.

At that moment the assistant came in. 'I say,' said the M.O. 'We've got a chap with remarkable eyesight here, would you like to test him?' The assistant looked out of the window and saw a car parked at extreme range on the parade ground. He asked Dick if he could tell the number. Fearing his bluff had at last been called Dick looked out. His luck held: it was his own car!"

Dick Bagnall-Oakeley (*anon*).

Apart from wartime service, which included the hazardous task of flying over enemy territory to photograph their aircraft on the ground, he remained at Gresham's School all his working life. Beyond the school walls he did much to promote the study of local wildlife among the wider East Anglian public, through his lectures, film shows and contributions to the BBC East television programmes. As well as a first-class photographer and film-maker, he was also a very talented artist. Upon his marriage in 1950, Dick moved into Brinton Hall, since when his son, Jeremy and his grandchildren have lived there. The extensive grounds and large lake have played host to a wide variety of birds including Spotted Crakes in 1950 and 1954, Ferruginous Duck in 1951, White-spotted Bluethroat in 1954 and Red-crested Pochards in 1959 and 1964.

The joy of spending time with D. B-O, as he was widely known, was not just his extensive knowledge of the local birdlife, he was also a great raconteur and I can still hear him recounting his delightful stories in a broad Norfolk accent, which he put on specially for the occasion.

Understandably Bernard Bishop was appointed as Assistant Warden on the Cley Reserve in 1972, after all in the 1950s and 1960s as a young lad he had helped his father, Billy, on the marsh, with such tasks as reed cutting and clearing dykes, as well as assisting Richard Richardson to catch birds in the Heligoland trap at Walsey Hills. Following his appointment, the additional manpower enabled the Norfolk Naturalists Trust to create new scrapes and erect additional hides overlooking them. When Billy retired in 1979, it was only natural that Bernard should take over as Warden, the third generation of Bishops to hold the post. During the early years of his tenure, Bernard planned and created a new drain passing northwards along the eastern edge of the reeds from the car park at the inland end of the East Bank. This increased security on the Reserve and prevented egg collectors from accessing the reed bed from the East Bank. He also established new, wider boardwalks allowing wheelchair access to the Reserve and replaced the existing 30-year old hides with larger more modern ones, despite the attempts of various North Sea surges from thwarting all his sterling work. He also moved back into Watcher's Cottage with his wife, Shirley, and their sons, where he had been born in 1949 and had spent his childhood years. In March 2019, Bernard retired as Warden after 47 years as an employee of the Norfolk Wildlife Trust, although he still assists the new Warden, George Baldock.

Bernard Bishop outside Watchers Cottage in 2015.

No account of the personalities of Cley would be complete without including Nancy Gull, whose café in Cley village was renowned throughout the British birding scene of the 1970s and '80s. Fortunately the years were recorded for posterity in a series of annual diaries, from which I included extracts in an article entitled 'The twitcher diaries' in the magazine *Birdwatch* in April 2015:

> I know that many readers of this article will have fond memories of Nancy's Café in Cley. Before the advent of bird lines and pagers, it was one of the only ways for birders, who were not on a local 'grapevine', to obtain up-to-date information as to the current location of local and national rarities. Sitting near the phone in Nancy's, having a quiet cup of coffee and a bun was simply not an option, as the phone would ring continuously as birders from all parts of Britain rang in to get the latest gen.

Eddy Myers answering the phone watched by Nancy Gull (*anon*).

Traditionally, Nancy's closed at the end of October and was only open at weekends during the winter months before re-opening full time at Easter. Despite this she still received frequent phone calls on weekdays in winter from birders seeking information. She was remarkably tolerant of this intrusion into her private life.

In August 1975, a hard-backed notebook was placed in Nancy's to be used as a diary, in which birds of interest seen in Norfolk could be recorded for the benefit of other birders and the County Bird Recorders, a tradition that continued without a break until the café closed in 1989. On moving from Cley to Sheringham, Jack and Nancy Gull, in whose house the café was situated, registered as patients with me, and Nancy subsequently gave me the diaries, instead of simply throwing them away! What a great loss of Cley's birding history that would have been. Since then they have sat on a shelf in my study, gathering dust, so it is a pleasure to share them again with the present generation of birders.

The first few entries in the 1975 diary were all written by 'JTC' (Tommy Corcoran) and relate to his records of sightings on Arnold's Marsh and from the Bittern Hide (how many of you can remember that particular hide?). Further down the page a walk from Cley to Blakeney Point on 10th August 1975 produced 20+ Pied Flycatchers and 2 Icterine Warblers as recorded by DJH [Dave Holman], SCJ [Steve Joyner], NW [Norman Williams] et al. By the third page records from Wells and even a Buff-breasted Sandpiper at Walberswick in Suffolk, were being included, and thereafter anything of note in East Anglia and further afield was added.

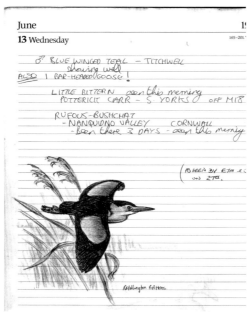

June   1!

13 Wednesday   165–20L

♂ BLUE WINGED TEAL — TITCHWELL
           showing well
ALSO 1 BAR-HEADED GOOSE !

LITTLE BITTERN seen this morning
   POTTERICK CARR – S YORKS ♂ off M18

RUFOUS-BUSHCHAT
   – NANQUIDNO VALLEY   CORNWALL
      – been there 3 DAYS – seen this morning

(AS BEEN 3½ ETH &c
(on 27th.

Little Bittern in Yorkshire by Richard Millington.

Many other now well-known names in the birding world recorded their observations in the first few pages, including John Marchant, Bill Sutherland and Chris Durdin (both in the UEA Bird Club), Tony Marshall (a frequent visitor to the north Norfolk coast from Essex), Chris Heard and Dudley Isles, to name but a few.

Almost inevitably, written records of bird sightings attract comments from other observers, who may question their authenticity, and Nancy's diaries were no exception. The first appeared on October 14th, during an unprecedented, at the time, arrival of Yellow-browed Warblers. One observer noted a Pallas's Warbler and 2 Yellow-browed Warblers at Wells, followed in parenthesis by 'some of the big boys saw 8 or more!' While a Cetti's Warbler at Walsey Hills in late October was considered 'not likely'. How things have changed! However, as time passed comments as innocuous as these began to become more barbed, but occasionally were amusing. For example, the entry for November 2nd reads: 'Lesser Grey Shrike & Short-toed Lark [at] Holme (take care to avoid minefield, barbed wire & machine gun post – the natives are hostile).

Some records are of momentous sightings in the history of Norfolk (and British) ornithology, such as the Fan-tailed Warbler seen only by Nick Dymond as it sang and displayed by the East Bank before flying purposefully west at 7.30 am on 24th August 1976, much to the chagrin of local observers. However, what was presumably the same bird was fortunately relocated at Holme five days later, where it continued to perform for the next 48 hours.

Although the first sketch (of a Greenish Warbler at Holme) appeared in early September 1976, it was not until 1980 that the first of Richard Millington's excellent line drawings in biro graced the pages of the diaries.

Tawny Pipit at Cley by Richard Millington.

In 1977, many more now familiar names began to appear in the diary, including one on May 29th by SJMG (Steve Gantlett, otherwise known as Captain Ticker), recording both Red-throated Pipit and Blue-headed Wagtail at Kelling Quags. While Eddie Myers' first entry was of a Red-backed Shrike, no less than 8 Icterine Warblers and a selection of other autumn migrants on Blakeney Point on August 7th. The very sad news of Richard Richardson's death was included on October 9th, although strangely enough the entry read: 'Dick passed away today', a name that he was known by to very few of his friends.

The adjudication of records by the self-appointed Cley Rarities Committee (CRC) first appeared following a sighting of a Black Kite over the Cley Road at Holt on November 5th, with the comment: 'Cley Rarities Committee finds this record totally unacceptable as the possibility of an escape cannot be ruled out and the veracity of the observer has been seriously questioned. However, the committee will reconsider if they see the bird in question.' In their defence the record was never submitted to the BBRC. Thereafter the words 'CRC rejected' appeared regularly in the diaries, in writing that looks suspiciously like that of Steve Gantlett!

On 28th May 1978, the infamous first-summer male Pied Wheatear (a new bird for the county) was found by Peter Allard at Winterton. For reasons which I never really understood, the record was suppressed and its arrival was passed on to only a few Norfolk birders, myself included although I was unable to travel to Winterton to see it.

By the following morning it had moved on, much to the annoyance of those who had failed to see it on the previous day.

A few days later, it became common knowledge and of those who had seen it, Dave Holman was particularly singled out as a 'conspirator', and the CRC made the following comments in Nancy's diary: 'Cley Records Committee herewith rejects D.J.Holman (ex-twitcher) for anti-social activities ie gross suppression' and 'As of this date anyone passing on information or in any way co-operating with P.Feakes, D.J.Holman or N.Williams will render themselves liable for trial and sentence by the Cley Rarities Committee'. It was clearly handbags at dawn!

In an attempt to deflect blame away from Dave Holman, Peter Allard on one of his infrequent visits to Cley wrote in the diary: 'Dave Holman was in no way responsible for the suppression of the male Pied Wheatear – East Coast Suppression Ltd.' Nevertheless, Dave was not allowed to forget about it for many years. Twitchers who 'dip out' on rare birds have very long memories!

As stated earlier, the first of Richard Millington's delightful line drawings in biro appeared in July 1980 and thereafter many of the rarities that turned up at Cley were recorded for posterity in this way in Nancy's diaries. Undoubtedly the most important was a fine sketch of Britain's only Rock Sparrow that was found by Steve Gantlett and Richard Millington along the beach fence on the Eye Field in the early morning of 14th June 1981, and which was seen by only three other observers. This diary page is also a good example of the sorts of comments that were prevalent at the time.

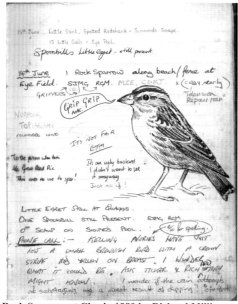

Rock Sparrow at Cley in 1980 by Richard Millington.

Occasionally Richard's sketches were executed in coloured crayons [as was shown on an earlier page]. Later diaries were also enlivened by the accurate drawings of Martin Elliott, who worked as an assistant warden at the Cley Reserve and often portrayed rarities from other parts of the country such as the long-staying second-winter Franklin's Gull at Porthleven in Cornwall in 1987. From the comments by the side of many of the sketches, there was clearly some artistic rivalry between him and Richard Millington, and it was not surprising that some of these drawings were removed from the diaries as trophies. Eddie Myers was obviously concerned about this and above the Franklin's Gull had written 'Please leave this drawing in the log'.

Franklin's Gull in Cornwall by Martin Elliott.

For over six months from October 1989, Norfolk hosted yet another British first in the form of a Red-breasted Nuthatch at Holkham that was portrayed by a variety of talented bird artists in the pages of Nancy's diaries. Fortunately it favoured the area around the royal family's summer house, where it often gave 'crippling views'.

Relevant and sometimes irrelevant newspaper cuttings began to appear in the diaries from the mid-1980s, including one of me in the stocks at Sheringham Carnival with Eddie Myers comment: 'It's what he deserves for suppressing the Alpine Accentor', a reference to one found and ringed by Kevin Shepherd near Dead Man's Wood nine years earlier! Someone else had written: 'Hang the bastard'. What it is to be popular!

The fame of Nancy's Café spread even further when an article about it appeared in the Sunday Express Magazine of October 1987 with a photo of Eddie Myers answering the phone watched over by Nancy (see page 44). The article began 'Nancy Gull, proprietress of Nancy's Café, has got used to the sight of her customers suddenly leaping to their feet and making a dash for the nearest exit without even pausing to pay their bills.'

Perhaps the most amusing entries relate to an unfortunate incident involving Tommy Corcoran, who along with Eddie Myers was one of the most regular contributors to the diaries from the very first one to the last in 1989. In early May 1987 Tommy decided to visit East Hills off Wells to look for migrants, hoping to find a Tawny Pipit. At high tide East Hills is an island but as the tide falls it is possible, with care, to wade across the channels and reach this isolated area of pines and scrub. Unfortunately, while attempting to cross one of the channels, Tommy lost his footing and fell into the water, losing his Hertel & Reuss telescope in the process, and nearly drowning.

The diary entry for May 8th reads: 'Tawny Corcoran. Pelagic Tours off Norfolk. In search of the underwater scope.' Two days later diary sketches illustrated 'Tommy Corcoran Birding Equipment' and included flippers, safety flares, snorkel, wet suit, periscope, water wings and spare clothing, while a week later a hand-drawn map appeared entitled 'Where not to watch birds in Norfolk (at high tide) by Tommy Corcoran'. This light-hearted banter continued until the end of the month, although Tommy did have the last laugh, when a Tawny Pipit was indeed found on East Hills on May 26th.

It was with great sadness that Nancy closed her café for good at the end of 1989, after providing birders, both local and from the far-flung corners of Britain, with sustenance and a welcome break, for 17 years. The final entry in that year's diary was of a Sooty Shearwater flying east off Blakeney Point on December 30th recorded by Phil Heath and Andy Stoddart. So ended an era at Cley.

Jack and Nancy Gull outside 'Nancy's Cafe', Cley in 1989 (*anon*).

Just think how much of the Norfolk birding folklore would have been lost if Nancy had simply thrown away the diaries, as she had intended. It just goes to show how important it is to retain written records and accounts from years gone by.

One of the first birders to move into Cley, and probably the most renowned, was Bryan Bland, who worked as a graphic designer but resigned as a Director of his company in 1974 and moved to Cley with his delightful wife, Betty. He bought the house, which had served as the local 'chippie' in Cley's High street and named it Flanders, as it had originally been the village slaughterhouse. From here Bryan and Betty ran residential birdwatching courses, which became world famous, as Bryan is a superb communicator and field ornithologist, and Betty's catering was first class. However, on one occasion her meal did not turn out quite as expected. During a particularly cold spell of weather one winter, Bryan had found the freshly dead corpse of a Bittern, and he decided that it would make an interesting basis for a casserole. The dish was duly prepared by Betty and served to their guests, but unfortunately it turned out to be as tough as old leather and inedible!

Bryan was also a Director of the birding holiday company Sunbird, and while living at Cley he also led tours to over 50 countries and ran over 1,000 courses. He was also an annual autumn visitor to the Isles of Scilly. His foreign exploits can be read in his highly amusing book *The Profit of Birding*.

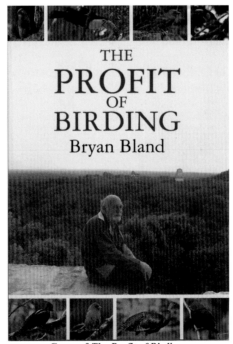

THE
PROFIT
OF
BIRDING
Bryan Bland

Cover of *The Profit of Birding*.

I was privileged to have been one of Bryan's friends and we went on many happy exploits together on birding trips in East Anglia, as well as taking part in several of the early *Country Life* bird races, as described in a later chapter. As an illustrator Bryan was eagerly sought after by budding authors of bird books and I was delighted when he agreed to illustrate my first book, *The birds of Sheringham*, published in 1987.

Front cover of *The birds of Sheringham*.

Wryneck at Dead Mans Wood from *The Birds of Sheringham* by Bryan Bland.

Sadly Betty Bland died in the 1990s and Bryan eventually moved to the south coast to live in Dorset. He is still sadly missed, having been one of the contemporary characters of the Cley birding scene.

Cley also attracted Steve Gantlett, aka 'Ticker', who changed from being an optician to a professional ornithologist, and who with Lee Evans, and Richard and Hazel Millington who also moved to Cley in the 1980s, established the Bird Information Service and published the monthly magazine *Birding World*, which ran from 1988 to 2013. Richard is another talented artist, who has illustrated many bird books and was the author and illustrator of *A Twitcher's Diary*. But along with

Richard Richardson, the most famous bird artist to move to Cley has been Robert Gillmor, who since 1988 has lived within sight of Richard's home at Hilltop. Robert has been a freelance wildlife artist since 1965 and along with Eric Ennion founded the Society of Wildlife Artists. His work has appeared in well over 100 books and in recent years he has specialised in linocuts that have been used as designs for the dust jackets of the *New Naturalist* series since 1985.

This is just a small selection of the many well-known birders who have decided to make Cley their home, others include Mark Golley, Tony Marr and Richard Porter.

*   *   *

Chapter 7

Councils, committees and other commitments

In Chapter 2, I described how I had become a bird ringer, an interest that lasted for well over half a century. It was also the start of my lifelong commitment to the work of the British Trust for Ornithology (BTO). As a young teenager thoughts of becoming a professional ornithologist were discouraged by my father, a retail pharmacist, who suggested that it would be a better to obtain a qualification that would guarantee work at the end, such as pharmacy or medicine. It was actually very sound advice for back in the 1950s there were very few appointments in which a knowledge of ornithology or even conservation was required, while a degree in biology almost inevitably meant a career in teaching, which at the time did not appeal.

As a youngster I had joined the RSPB's Junior Bird Recorders' Club, which subsequently became the Young Ornithologists' Club (YOC), but it was only when I joined the BTO in 1960 that I really felt that I was making a small but valuable contribution to 'proper' ornithology, rather than just being a 'birdwatcher'. Herein lies the great strength of the BTO, in that it allows amateurs to take part in a variety of ornithological projects under the guidance of its expert, professional staff.

It was thanks to the BTO and Bob Spencer, one of my ringing trainers, that I was able to join the team that visited Morocco in 1965 to ring spring migrants as they completed their trans-Saharan migration, en route to their breeding grounds in Europe. The month long expedition to North Africa certainly stimulated my interest in bird migration and so it was perhaps not surprising that on moving to Norfolk in 1969, I sought out a coastal ringing site to further this interest. However, ringing was not the only aspect of BTO fieldwork with which I became involved: I was soon contributing to the Nest Record Scheme, as well as covering some 10-km squares for the BTO's first Atlas of Breeding Birds, which in East Norfolk was overseen by the BTO's Regional Representative John Goldsmith. who at the time was working in the Natural History Department of the Castle Museum in Norwich. In addition to birds, John had a great interest and expertise in bats, and was latterly known as 'Norfolk's Batman'.

John Goldsmith by his beloved Land Rover (*Sue Goldsmith*).

When John decided to stand down as BTO Regional Rep for East Norfolk in 1978, I agreed to take on the role, as an interim measure, but in the event I continued for the next 13+ years! Only a year later I found myself on BTO Council, which continued for the next six years. At that time Council meetings, under the chairmanship of John McMeeking, were held in London. It was daunting enough to find myself on BTO Council, let alone sitting in the august council chamber of the Zoological Society of London at Regent's Park Zoo, where the meetings were held. In fact I was so overawed at my first meeting that I didn't utter a single word, which may come as a surprise to friends who know me now! Later meetings were held in the computer room at the BTO's headquarters at Beech Grove, Tring, where we sat surrounded by large, flat tins of reel upon reel of computer tapes, which stored all the BTO archives.

Prior to 1979, all the BTO records were stored on paper or cards, but in that year the Trust purchased its first computer, and Dick Newell and Chris Mead wrote a suite of programs that met the BTO's needs. That first BTO computer occupied a fair part of the Computer Room at Beech Grove and all the data had to be stored on the tapes. From then on, there was no looking back, aided by the computer expertise of the recently appointed Director, Raymond O'Connor. I can well remember sitting next to him at lunch at one of the Swanwick Conferences, listening bemused as he tried to explain to me the extraordinary possibilities of Word Processing.

Beech Grove at Tring (*Stanley Howe*).

I thoroughly enjoyed my time on BTO Council, not least because it gave me the opportunity to meet many of the leading lights in British ornithology, even though it meant almost monthly trips from Norfolk to Tring to attend meetings of the Trust, especially during the three years that I was Honorary Secretary and the one year I filled in as Honorary Treasurer. My wife was remarkably tolerant of my frequent absences on BTO business, especially as I was still acting as the BTO Regional Rep, not only for East Norfolk, but for a couple of years for the whole of the county. During this time local BTO Conferences needed to be arranged at the University of East Anglia, which meant various speakers became house guests for the weekend, including Ian (D.I.M) Wallace, Chris Mead, Peter Lack and Kevin (Jeff) Baker.

The BTO's Annual Conference at The Hayes Conference Centre in Swanwick, Derbyshire was one of the highlights of the year and I looked forward with keen anticipation to the weekend, both for the camaraderie and the informative lectures, not forgetting to mention the drinking into the early hours and the games of table tennis with Kent legend, Bob Scott. In 1986 I was privileged, on behalf of the Trust, to present the Bernard Tucker Medal to fellow ringer, Mike Boddy, for his contribution to the Constant Effort Site ringing programme. I felt even more honoured when I was presented with the BTO's Jubilee Medal at the Annual Conference in 1988 for my 'committed devotion to the Trust'.

The author presenting the Tucker Medal to Mike Boddy (*Tim Davis*).

I became particularly friendly with BTO staff member, Kevin Baker, due to our common interests in both ringing and golf. When he retired from the BTO after 47 years of dedicated service, I was delighted to be able to write a tribute to his contributions to the work of the Trust, which was published in *BTO News* and *LifeCycle*. He had worked in almost every BTO department, including 29 years in the Ringing Unit, and latterly as Head of Marketing. Away from work he has always been a keen sportsman, including fishing, cricket, golf, karate, and a skydiving photographer, which almost cost him his life. To most people he is known as Jeff, but to me he will always be Kevin. In 1991, when the BTO moved from Tring to The Nunnery at Thetford and for reasons known only to him, he decided to change his name from Kevin (by which he was known to staff and members) to Jeff. Actually he was simply reverting to his given name of Jeffery. I shall never forget the annual BTO Conference where members first came across the 'new' Jeff Baker. As a joke several of us also changed our name badges so that our first names were Jeff; it quickly caught on and by the end of the weekend conference there were more than a hundred Jeffs in attendance!

Jeff (Kevin) Baker in Majorca (*anon*).

But the one member of staff whose name will always be associated with the BTO was Chris Mead, who very sadly died in January 2003, at the comparatively young age of 62. His contribution to the work of the Trust was vast, as I explained in my In the Countryside column in the *Eastern Daily Press* of 9th February 2003:

> With the sudden death of Chris Mead in January, the birding world has lost one of its most loved, respected and knowledgeable members.
>
> In recent years, it was to Chris that the national and local press turned for information or comment on topical birding matters, and despite having retired from the BTO in 1994, on health grounds, he remained the Trust's spokesman on a wide range of topics.
>
> Some indication of his vast knowledge can be assessed from the books that he contributed to and wrote. Perhaps the two for which he will best be remembered are *Bird Migration*, published in 1983 and more recently, *State of the Nation's Birds*. But it was in the field of bird ringing that Chris made his major contribution to the work of the BTO.
>
> Chris first joined the staff in 1961, working in the Ringing Office, which at that time was just a single small room in the section of the Natural History Museum in South Kensington known as the Bird Room. The head of the ringing scheme, at the time, was the irrepressible Bob Spencer, who also became a legend during his lifetime.
>
> With the appointment of Chris Mead to the staff, the available space in the office became appreciably less (he was always larger than life, in all senses of the word). Whether or not this was one of the deciding factors, it was Chris, in autumn 1962, who was sent on a foray to Tring, his ancestral homeland, to seek out possible alternative accommodation, and there he discovered Beech Grove. Within a year the Trust had moved into its new home, where it remained until transferring to Thetford in 1991.
>
> There must have been few major ringing projects with which Chris was not closely involved, for ringing was not only his work, it was also his hobby. As a member of the Cambridge Bird Club, he joined the Wash Wader Ringing Group and was a keen participant in the group's many adventures.
>
> When the Sand Martin Enquiry was launched in the 1960s, Chris and his recently married bride 'V' took their summer holiday catching Sand Martins in Scotland. Their final tally was a staggering 2344 birds ringed and 78 birds already carrying rings, the vast majority from colonies over 200 miles away, including four from France.
>
> In recent years, he concentrated his efforts on tits, Pied Flycatchers in Wales, and nearer to home the establishment of the Wissey Ringing Group.
>
> Chris will be very greatly missed by everyone who was fortunate enough to have known him and our thoughts are with his family at this sad time.

Another organisation with which I became closely involved on moving to Norwich in 1970 was the Norfolk & Norwich Naturalists' Society, the county's oldest natural history organisation, founded in 1869. One of its roles is to publish the Annual *Norfolk Bird & Mammal Report* (jointly with the Norfolk Naturalists' Trust until 1982) and in 1973 I was invited to join the editorial team, writing the migration report for the Cley and Salthouse area for that year. In 1980, John Bruhn, who had been responsible for the ringing section in the annual Bird Report for 10 years (having succeeded Richard Richardson), retired from the editorial committee and I took over the compilation and writing of the Ringing Report. John's knowledge of all aspects of bird ringing within the county was invaluable, as was his interpretation and comments on the individual recoveries. His was a very hard act to follow and I continued in this role until 1988 when Allan Hale took over. For the next 23 years Allan compiled the Annual Ringing Report, which was no mean achievement, as at that time, all the recovery details had to be obtained from the individual ringers. Subsequently, it became a lot easier and less time consuming once the more notable recoveries were freely available on the BTO website. Following the untimely death in 2017 of Steve Wakeham, who had taken over from Allan Hale, ringing recoveries involving Norfolk have unfortunately no longer appeared in the annual *Norfolk Bird Report*.

The first published *Norfolk Bird Report* covered the year 1953. Prior to this the more interesting county records appeared in an annual publication entitled *Wild Bird Protection in Norfolk* a report by the Council of the Norfolk Naturalists' Trust. The Editor of the 1953 Report was Michael Seago, assisted by the Records Committee consisting of Ted Ellis, Richard Richardson and Archie Daukes (after whom Daukes Hide on the Cley Reserve is named). Michael continued in this role for the next 45 years, a unique record as the Editor of a county bird report. Up to 1975, the authenticity of the scarcer Norfolk species (not rare enough nationally for consideration by the British Birds Rarities Committee) was decided by Michael Seago and Richard Richardson. But in that year a County Records Committee was established comprising Peter Allard, Giles Dunmore, Dave Holman, Steve Joyner and me, and our remit was to adjudicate on the submitted descriptions of records of semi-rarities and more common species out of normal season or range. A list of those species for which descriptions were required, *unless* they had been seen by three or more observers, appeared in the 1975 Annual Report and the list was updated as and when necessary. I have to say that I found it extremely difficult to decide whether records should be accepted or not, and I fully sympathise with the current members of the County Records Committee, even though most of my records of description species are now rejected! I have never been good at writing descriptions of birds that I have seen, and as most of my birding is carried out alone, no one else is present to verify my sightings. Over the years I have seen almost 3,500 species worldwide, including over 90% of those on the British List, but as I depend heavily on the 'jizz' of a bird to identify it, which is very hard to put into words, many of my records are considered 'not proven'. Such is life. Thank goodness for digital photography.

Living only a few miles along the coast from Cley, I have naturally spent more time at that Norfolk Wildlife Trust (NWT) Reserve, than at any of the other Trust Reserves in Broadland or the Brecks. Over the 50+ years that I have been visiting Cley, I have seen great changes on the Reserve itself, in the number of visiting birders and the equipment that is now available. As my partner, Robina Churchyard says, many people look more like decorated Christmas trees as they walk around encumbered by binoculars, a telescope mounted on a tripod, a camera with a telephoto lens, and more often than not a mobile phone and/or a pager, not to mention a parabolic reflector if they are keen on recording bird songs and calls.

When I first started visiting Cley, the few hides were very small and access on to the Reserve was not possible before 10am and not at all on a Monday. However, it was possible to obtain almost open access by becoming a Life Fellow of the Norfolk Naturalists Trust, as it was then known. But this was a fairly expensive option, and as I understand it, there were only ever two Life Fellows: Peter Kitchener and me. On the back of the membership card it stated that it was 'Invalid Without A Photograph'. Peter and I took out our Life Fellowships in 1981, and at that time I was sporting a moustache, the one and only time in my life when I have had one, and then only for a few months. So the photo on the card bore very little resemblance to me during the ensuing years that I used it!

One of only two Life Fellows.

I accompanied Peter Kitchener on many birding trips over the years, both in Norfolk and further afield, and it was with great sadness in 2008 that I learnt he had been diagnosed with multiple myeloma from which he tragically died eight years later. I was highly honoured to be asked by his family to say a few words about our friendship at his funeral service in 2016, and some extracts from that tribute follow:

> Peter was always very precise in everything that he did and so it has turned out that I first met him exactly 50 years ago in September 1966. I had travelled up to Cley for a week's holiday with my school friend Mike Bowtell, and we were camping by the Beach Road at Cley. In adjoining tents were Peter and Robin Hamilton and we very quickly struck up a friendship that would turn out to be lifelong.
>
> Exactly five years earlier, in September 1961, Peter had made a name for himself by finding a Sharp-tailed Sandpiper, known in those days as a Siberian Pectoral Sandpiper, at Bedford sewage farm, while out birding with his friends from Bedford School, including Nick Dymond. In order to have the record ratified, they contacted James Ferguson-Lees, who in turn took along Ian Wallace to confirm the identification. Much to Peter's disappointment, despite having been one of the original finders, the record was credited to Fergie-Lees and D.I.M. Wallace in the British Birds Rarity Committee Report.
>
> Peter had been an active member of the RSPB's Junior Bird Recorders' Club, submitting records and notes over several years, along with the likes of Paul Dukes, Bill Harvey (Kent), Alan Kitson, Norman Sills (ex-warden and creator of the wetlands at Titchwell & Lakenheath) and Dave Holman, all birders who would make their mark in the future. In 1962 Peter presented a short paper at the JBRC's Annual Conference held at the RSPB HQ at The Lodge, Sandy entitled 'Constructive Ornithology in Bedfordshire', quite a title for a young teenager. He was also awarded third place in the Salzman Prize for field skills.

However, it wasn't only birds in which Peter was interested, he was extremely enthusiastic and knowledgeable about butterflies, moths and dragonflies, and like me was trying to get to grips with the identification of bumble bees. He was a Life Fellow of the Norfolk Wildlife Trust & a Life Member of the British Dragonfly Society. He was also a very keen and competent wildlife photographer, particularly of insects.

As I said, we first met in 1966, and I was delighted when I moved to Norfolk in 1969 to discover that he was working at the Norfolk & Norwich Hospital. Two years later I joined him at the N&N as a Medical Registrar and it was only natural that it was with Peter that I should go out to celebrate the birth of my first son, Chris, strangely enough exactly 44 years ago yesterday. Peter was always keen on his food (and wine) and I remember we both enjoyed Lobster Thermidor at the Pig & Whistle in Norwich, or as we knew it then the Wig & Pistle! I think that it was at about this time that Peter made his one and only foray into General Practice. One thing that put him off was the thought that all 4,000 patients registered with the practice would become ill at the same time when he was on call at night! But he was lacking the most important attribute of a GP – his writing was both neat and legible!

Over the years, Peter and I enjoyed many enjoyable days out together, birding in Norfolk and the photo on the back of the Service sheet was on just such a day, when he came to help me ring birds at Dead Man's Wood in Sheringham. Jays are renowned for being very aggressive in the hand, and have fairly sharp and strong bills. As I needed a photo of a Jay in the hand, I asked Peter to hold it, knowing only too well that it would probably have a go at him. Somehow he worked his magic and it sat perfectly still! I also seem to remember that he wore the same jumper, as in that photo, for many years and no doubt Jan can remember it too.

Peter Kitchener holding a Jay at Dead Man's Wood.

In 2007, I was taking a small group of birders to Panama, and Peter decided to join us, it would have been our first trip abroad together. In the event it wasn't to be, as he was suffering from the first symptoms of myeloma, although it was not diagnosed until the following year, and unfortunately he had to pull out. Despite the debilitating effect of both the illness and the treatment, Peter never let it affect his enthusiasm for going out birding, and I know that in the last few years he particularly appreciated the help and companionship of Dave Holman & Christine, and John & Judy Geeson, who herself tragically died from cancer only last year.

Knowing that his days were numbered, Peter was determined to see as many species as possible in the time remaining, and it is a great tribute to his determination that he was able to see no less than 265 species last year in East Anglia.

The last full day I spent with him in the field was October 15th last year, and we were joined by Mike Bowtell, who was over from Ireland, and his brother David. We had an unforgettable day out together walking around the woods at Wells and Holkham, and seeing the Red-flanked Bluetail, Humes & Pallas's Warblers. On the day, my knee was playing up from too much time spent on the golf course, Mike was troubled with sciatica and his brother David, who is nearly 80, was suffering from gout, so the three of us were hobbling along, not so Peter who was striding out in front determined to see all the goodies, in fact he appeared to be the only fit one amongst us!

I last saw Peter at Abbey Farm, Flitcham on January 13th this year, of course wearing his trade mark floppy green hat, and we were both blessed with superb views of the Pallid Harrier as it glided past us. Peter sadly told me that he had virtually run out of treatment options but despite this was remarkably positive and philosophical, as he had been for the last eight years.

To separate him from other friends called Peter, I always referred to him as Peter Kitch, but I'd be surprised if anyone was less kitsch than Peter. He was always great company with a wry sense of humour. For someone to have put up with me for 50 years, with my constant chatter and quirky sense of humour, he must have been very special, and Peter certainly was that.

Only five years earlier another birding friend, Simon Aspinall, had died after bravely fighting the ravaging effects of motor neurone disease. Although he is best remembered for his conservation work in the United Arab Emirates, he had many connections with Norfolk, not least having graduated from the University of East Anglia, as well as having a home in Cley. In his memory the Norfolk Wildlife Trust named their new building the Simon Aspinall Wildlife Education Centre, where courses and workshops are now held. In November 2015, I ran a six-week course entitled A Beginners' Guide to Norfolk Birds, consisting of two talks in the morning on bird behaviour and identification, followed by an afternoon visit to the Reserve. It was fully booked and in the following April, an intermediate course was arranged for the same group, covering the less common Norfolk birds. A similar course was arranged for the next year, after which Julian Thomas took over as tutor. I found it most satisfying to see how the identification skills of the participants improved as the course went on, and I know that several of them have become very keen and competent birders.

Fund raising has always been important to the NWT and in March 1990, five of us found a novel way of supporting an appeal to help purchase some of Norfolk's woods and meadows that were under threat from development. We all were bearded and at a crowded Crown Inn at Sheringham one evening, we had half our beards shaved off by the assembled drinkers and agreed to remain like this for the next 24 hours. I dread to think what my patients must have thought of me in the surgery the next day but it was all well worthwhile as between us we managed to raise £1200 for the woods and meadows appeal.

Half beard shave at The Crown (*Fran Taylor*).

As a member of the Councils of both the NWT and the Norfolk & Norwich Naturalists' Society in the early 1990s, I met many of the major land owners in the county, which proved invaluable when it came to seeking permission to carry out fieldwork on the big estates for the local and national bird atlas projects. In 2016, I was amazed to learn that I had been awarded the Norfolk Wildlife Trust's Sydney Long Medal for services to nature conservation in Norfolk. I felt highly honoured to have been proposed for this most prestigious award, especially in the Trust's 90th anniversary year.

Tony Leach presenting the author with the Sydney Long Medal (*Robina Churchyard*).

Since January 2015 my main interest has revolved around the activities of the North East Norfolk Bird Club (NENBC). Fortuitously its formation coincided with my stopping ringing, and I was pleased to have an alternative to capture my interest. The Club was the brainchild of Trevor Williams and Phil Hall and was established to 'bring together people with a love and concern for birds in [the north-east corner of Norfolk], to share knowledge and information, encourage participation in exploring our rich wildlife heritage and promote awareness of our threatened natural environment'. The Club has certainly been a great success, as is demonstrated by the steadily growing membership that currently stands at 360, after only five years. Members are encouraged to submit all of their bird sightings in the Club area and the number of such records on the Club website reached 300,000 during 2020. A variety of long-term data gathering projects have been set up, including the comparative annual abundance of the commoner species in both summer and winter, and an autumn co-ordinated sea-watch from various coastal localities.

As with any project, feedback to participants is vitally important and this is achieved through a monthly electronic Newsletter, *The Pied Flyer*, professionally edited by the Club Secretary, Carol Thornton. Many members make regular contributions and amongst those that I have written have been two series entitled 'Bird of the Month' and 'Tricky Dicky!', the latter explaining the differences in the appearance of similarly-looking species, such as Dunlin and Curlew Sandpiper, and Reed and Lapland Buntings. Finally, one Club project that commenced in 2017, has involved members recording the song periods of the commoner birds, to see if the timing of bird song has changed in response to recent climate change. The results from 2018 and 2019 have been written up and we hope that they will be published in *British Birds* in 2021.

*   *   *

Chapter 8

Birding abroad

Since my first foreign holiday to Majorca as a 13-year old in 1956, I have been lucky enough to visit over 50 countries and overseas territories on every continent except for Antarctica. While most of the early trips were taken as family holidays, many of those in the last 30 years have been specifically for birding: as a participant on an organised tour, on a privately arranged visit with a local guide or as a tour leader. Also over a period of 12 years I was fortunate enough to be a guest lecturer on a variety of cruises that visited northern Europe, the Baltic and the Americas, the highs and lows of which are recounted in the next two chapters. Included in this one are just a few of the highlights of my many foreign adventures.

My appetite for foreign birding had been wetted by the BTO ringing trip to Morocco in 1965, and this was followed three years later by a holiday with my old school friend, Mike Bowtell, to Majorca, where we saw for the first time three of the eponymous birds on the island: Eleonora's Falcon, Audouin's Gull and Marmora's Warbler. However, being single and in our early twenties, it wasn't only the feathered birds that caught our attention! The following year, Mike and I again joined forces and spent a most enjoyable fortnight camping in the Camargue in southern France, an area that I had previously visited in 1962 with Mike Hyde, another friend from school. It was extremely useful to refresh my memory on the finer identification features of the breeding birds of the Mediterranean region, which was put to good use, only a week after returning home to Norfolk, when a Great Reed Warbler turned up at Cantley.

After getting married in 1970, my only foreign trips during the next 20 years were family holidays to destinations that included the Greek island of Cephallonia, Halkidiki on the Greek mainland, France and Florida. The last made an ideal introduction to trans-Atlantic birding, at the same time as enabling my wife and young sons to enjoy the delights of Disney World, Epcot Centre and the Kennedy Space Centre. Not that I didn't also have great fun at these world-famous holiday attractions. In the same way, a family holiday to The Gambia in spring 1991, staying at the Sunwing Hotel at Bakau, was the perfect way to combine a beach holiday with an introduction to African birds. In fact, I enjoyed the African experience so much that I returned to The Gambia in December, as leader of a birding trip organised by the local travel agent, and again in the following two years, with my good friend from Suffolk, Derek Moore, as co-leader on the third trip. An amusing incident happened at the end of one of the trips, as I described in the Norfolk & Norwich Naturalists' Society quarterly bulletin *The Norfolk Natterjack* under the title 'Illegal immigrants from West Africa':

> On the night before we were due to fly home, I left my trainers outside on the veranda, in order for them to dry out before I packed them in my luggage the following morning. As is my usual habit when packing, the next day I stuffed them with dirty socks and other items needing to be washed, and deposited them in my suitcase.

A couple of days after returning home, I decided to give the trainers a clean and took them into the garden to shake out any sand and other debris, and to my surprise, what should fall out but two West African Toads!

Not being sure what the position was regarding their importation, I phoned Norwich airport and was told that quarantine was not necessary and that I had probably not broken any laws. The problem then was what to do with them! With his veterinary knowledge and contacts at London Zoo, Ian Keymer was the obvious person to contact and he duly rang up one of the curators at the zoo. Although they had no West African Toads, financial restraints prevented the addition of any more animals to their collection. Janet Keymer came to the rescue and the toads became part of the menagerie at Gresham's Prep School.

In the same way, a holiday to Trinidad & Tobago with my wife, Fran, in 1997, led on to me being asked to take over a birding trip to these two beautiful, bird rich islands, two years later. Geoff Gibbs, who had been leading trips there for several years, became ill and asked if I could take his place. I didn't need a second invitation! As with all the foreign birding holidays that I led, it soon became apparent that they are far from holidays for the leader, and on occasions I felt I needed a proper rest when I returned home and was faced with a surgery full of patients. While it is most enjoyable showing tour participants the exotic birds that are encountered, often the greatest problems revolve around the logistics, such as transport, accommodation, liaising with the local guides and most important of all ensuring that everyone gets on well (there is nearly always one person on a trip that tries the leader's patience). I believe that some of the folk who came abroad with me, did so because I was a doctor, and they felt that if any of their chronic medical problems flared up, they would be adequately cared for! On the trips to The Gambia, which seemed to attract the old and infirm, I held a 'surgery' in my room immediately after breakfast on most days, before setting off to our destination for the day. However, these trips did provide me with material for my In the Countryside columns in the *Eastern Daily Press*, such as the two that follow, the first on Trinidad:

> I've recently returned from a birdwatching trip to Trinidad and Tobago, the two most southerly islands in the Caribbean chain. Although politically a single unit, the two islands are very different, as far as the birds are concerned.
>
> Trinidad lies only seven miles off the coast of Venezuela and geologically is part of South America. Half of the island is forested, and in the north, where we stayed, there is a range of low mountains, peaking at just over 3,000 feet. For a comparatively small island (under 2,000 square miles) the diversity of wildlife is amazing.
>
> Perhaps the most famous birds of Trinidad are the Scarlet Ibises. A must for any visitor to the island has to be a boat trip on the mangrove swamp at Caroni. While slowly passing along the narrow channels, through the otherwise impenetrable red mangroves, the keen-eyed boatman pointed out a whole range of wildlife.

Cayman, small members of the alligator family, slid silently beneath the surface as the boat approached; while Cook's tree boas, one of the many species of snake in Trinidad (most of which are non-poisonous), garlanded themselves around the branches of the mangroves.

As we approached the more open areas of water in the middle of the swamp, the first few flights of Scarlet Ibis began to appear. Dazzlingly red birds, related to the herons, flew low over us in line astern, in parties of up to thirty.

As the sun began to set and the sky turned orange, more and more arrived to roost in the safety of the extensive and inaccessible mangroves. Perhaps surprisingly, many of these birds make the daily return journey from feeding grounds in Venezuela.

Nestling amongst the rain forest of the Northern Range is the world-famous Asa Wright Nature Centre. An absolute paradise for birdwatchers and indeed naturalists of any persuasion. Here we stayed in the comfortably furnished lodge, originally built as the estate-house.

Each day began at 6 am with coffee on the veranda while watching the first arrivals at the feeding stations below. Chestnut Woodpeckers and various species of tanager voraciously attacked the bananas, pineapple slices and other fruit put out daily for the birds. Hummingbirds and honeycreepers drank from the feeders filled with sugared water, while Channel-billed Toucans with their outrageously large bills, delicately picked fruit from the trees of the nearby rain forest. Despite visiting Trinidad during the wet season, we were very fortunate with the weather; but when it rained - boy did it rain!

And the second column on our visit to Tobago read:

A few months ago, I described some of the highlights of a visit I made to Trinidad in July. During the same trip I also spent three days on its smaller sister island of Tobago.

The short flight from Trinidad to Tobago takes only about 20 minutes, but the scenery, culture and birdlife of the two islands is quite different. If it's possible, Tobago is even more laid back than Trinidad and being much smaller, the beautiful, deep azure-blue sea is visible from most parts of the island.

We stayed at the Blue Waters Inn at Speyside, a charming bay at the north-eastern corner of the island. As elsewhere in the Caribbean, many of the birds are remarkably tame and meal times are often spent in their company. Bananaquits, small black and yellow birds, are regular visitors to dining areas, where they share your fruit juice, fresh fruits and even sugar from the sugar bowl.

Bananaquit.

Many of the flowering shrubs in the hotel grounds attract diminutive hummingbirds. The males often appear uniformly dark, until the light catches their iridescent plumage at the right angle. Then instantly they become transformed into real gems, none more so than the Ruby-topaz Hummingbird with its brilliant orange breast.

The national bird of Tobago is the Rufous-vented Chachalaca. A brown game bird, the size of a small turkey, which has a very loud and persistent call. Groups of them can often be heard calling from the forest around the hotel, particularly at dawn! Incidentally, the name chachalaca is onomatopoeic, as are cuckoo and curlew.

But, for me, the highlight of our trip was a visit to the small offshore island of Little Tobago. Our transport was a glass-bottomed boat, which we boarded at the hotel quay. During the short sea crossing we saw many colourful fish around the coral, clearly visible through the glass hull.

Little Tobago is uninhabited by man, but is home to a large colony of seabirds. Perhaps, the most attractive are the Red-billed Tropicbirds, tern-like birds with incredibly long tail streamers, making them so elegant in flight. One pair had nested only a few feet from the path and we were able to photograph the well-grown nestling at arm's length!

But the highlight of the trip was a Terek Sandpiper, a new species for Trinidad and Tobago and only the fourth for the Neotropics. In view of its rarity, an account of the circumstances surrounding its finding was published in *Cotinga* the journal of the Neotropical Bird Club:

Accompanied by Kenny Calderon (a local guide), a small group of British birders and I visited Trinidad and Tobago, in June –July 1999. On the second day of the trip, 28 June, we were greeted with torrential rain but undeterred we set off for the mudflats at Waterloo. Near the coast, the rain got even heavier, and the roads and fields began to flood.

Eventually KC announced that we would try to observe shorebirds from a fishing shelter at the edge of flats. To our great surprise, the shelter proved to be an ideal site to scan the shore. Attention finally turned to the smaller shorebirds, some of which required careful scrutiny. Kenny pointed out a party of c.20 Semipalmated Sandpipers *Calidris pusilla*, among which I found a few Western Sandpipers *C. mauri*.

After c. 20 minutes Peter Wild announced that he had found a bird resembling a Terek Sandpiper *Xenus cinereus*, a species that was known to him solely from field guide illustrations. I regarded this identification as extremely unlikely, but when Terry Marshall located the individual and asked me to study it, I soon realised that PW's original suspicions were entirely correct! KC had, unsurprisingly, never even heard of the species. Realising that it was almost certainly a first record for Trinidad and Tobago, and possibly the Caribbean, I began to make careful mental notes of the relevant features, while trying to ensure that all members of the group saw it. Unfortunately, during the ten minutes that it was under scrutiny, it frequently disappeared behind some vegetation. There was, however, no doubt of the identification; I have previously seen three in England (where it is also rare), one at Eilat, Israel, and six in Goa, India.

This was followed by a description of the bird, and the record was subsequently accepted by the Trinidad & Tobago Rare Birds Committee. Fortunately the rain stopped in mid-afternoon and as described in the first excerpt given above, we ended a most successful day with a memorable (and dry!) boat trip with James Madoo on Caroni Swamp. For most of the party the Scarlet Ibises or Red-capped Cardinals eclipsed the Terek Sandpiper, as birds of the day!!

My first visit to South America was in November 2000 on a Naturetrek holiday with Andy Tucker as tour leader, and it provided good copy for three of my In the Countryside columns in the *Eastern Daily Press*, from which some extracts follow:

…Although small, Ecuador, a country named after its position on the equator, is a land of great contrasts. One day we were in a steamy Amazonian rain forest and the next on a cold and bleak Andean mountain top at over 14,000 feet.

After flying into Quito, the country's capital, which itself is situated at 9,000 feet, we spent a couple of days acclimatizing, before making for the higher passes. The scenery here was majestic. Surrounded, as we were, by towering cloud forest-covered mountains, as far as the eye could see. On one memorable morning we rose before dawn to watch the sun rise from behind the snow covered peak of the volcano Antisana. At over 17,000 feet it is one of the highest points in Ecuador and the sight of the sun reflecting off the deep snow is a memory I shall forever cherish.

The bird life was rich and varied with different species appearing as we climbed higher and higher. Perhaps the most striking were the brilliantly coloured mountain-tanagers, their names describing well their beautiful appearance, such as the Scarlet-bellied and the Blue-winged Mountain-tanagers. We crossed many fast-flowing torrents, the water cutting through deep mountain gorges eventually to feed the mighty Amazon.

One bird that we all wanted to see was the Torrent Duck, a species that has adapted to these raging mountain rivers. Incredibly, our sharp-eyed local guide Pancho spotted one on a riverside rock several hundred feet below the road on which we were travelling. It was a fine drake with brown upperparts, and a black and white striped head. Through the telescope we were able to appreciate the skill of this superbly adapted bird as it expertly dived into the fast flowing turbulent water, to reappear twenty seconds later as it climbed out on to another boulder.

Travelling ever higher we came to the desolate and inhospitable paramo, an area lying above the tree line. Here all the vegetation is stunted and few birds are to be found. We were very fortunate to locate a pair of the much sought-after Rufous-bellied Seedsnipe feeding nearby amongst the tussocks. Despite behaving and looking very much like grouse, seedsnipe are placed in a family of their own. Although we failed to see an Andean Condor we left this part of Ecuador more than happy with the long list of birds that we had encountered.

...the second half of our trip took us into the Amazonian basin, where the tropical rainforests cover an amazing 2.5 million square miles that are inhabited by an awe inspiring variety of birds, plants, insects and mammals.

Our base was to be Sacha Lodge, a 5,000-acre reserve where Andy Tucker, had worked for a year previously. After a short flight over the Andes from Quito, we landed at the town of Puerto Francisco de Orellano, named after the Spanish lieutenant-general who is accredited with discovering the Amazon. From here we boarded a motorised canoe for the 50-mile trip along the River Napo, the major tributary of the River Amazon. We were soon spotting the typical birds of this riverine habitat, such as Black Caracara, Yellow-billed and Large-billed Terns, as well as Ospreys and Spotted Sandpipers, both winter visitors from North America.

Spotted Sandpiper.

On arrival at the reserve we still had to cross Lake Pilchicocha by dugout canoe to reach Sacha Lodge. What a setting! Buildings constructed solely from local materials, surrounded on all sides by dense tropical rain forest and the beautiful Lake Pilchicocha, home to caimans, electric eels and piranhas, which we were assured were vegetarian!

One of the highlights of a stay at Sacha is a morning spent in the treetop hide, which stands 140 feet high and is built around a giant kapok tree. From the viewing platform a unique insight into the bird life of the canopy is possible. A constant stream of brightly-coloured tanagers flitted from tree to tree, including some really special ones such as Paradise, Masked Crimson and Golden Tanagers to name but three species. A pair of Cream-coloured Woodpeckers was particularly beautiful while the White-throated Toucans displayed a stunning mixture of colours. The haunting cries of a pair of Laughing Falcons, with red howler monkeys calling in the distance, made for an unforgettable experience.

Back at the lake, we searched for another speciality of the lowland waterways of the northern Neotropics, the Hoatzin. We soon located two clambering through the waterside vegetation. Over two feet in length and with a long, shaggy crest, they really were some of the most bizarre-looking birds that I have ever seen.

One of the great delights (and frustrations) of birding in a new continent for the first time is seeing species that bear no relationship or similarity in appearance to the familiar birds back home. Such was certainly the case on my first trip to Australia in 2011. Unfortunately I am unable to remember exactly how I came to know Tony Dymond, the expat brother of the well-known British birder, Nick Dymond, but he was a wonderfully helpful person for my first visit 'down under'. He lives in New South Wales, and part of the deal was that I should give a presentation to the Cumberland Bird Club, of which he was one of the Officers. The following is an account of our four-week trip in November 2011, as it appeared in the *Cumberland Bird Club Newsletter*:

It never rains in Australia, or at least that was what I was led to believe, and I would have agreed until the last week of our month-long visit to your wonderful country in November 2011.

It was way back in April that Tony Dymond kindly helped us to put together an itinerary for Robina & me to enjoy the avian delights of New South Wales, and for the first three weeks we certainly weren't disappointed. The final week was a different story but more of that later.

The long flight from England was made more tolerable by a three-day stopover in Singapore, our first visit to South-east Asia. This was an opportunity to familiarise ourselves with some of the commoner and more brightly-coloured birds of the region, such as Blue-tailed Bee-eater, Stork-billed Kingfisher & Pink-necked Green Pigeon. All species aptly named for their distinctive features.

Stork-billed Kingfisher (*Robina Churchyard*).

We arrived in Brisbane after an overnight flight and by mid-morning were installed in the Watermark Hotel, conveniently overlooking the Roma Street Parkland. Now the fun would begin! The first day birding on a new continent is like starting all over again and it took me back to my early birdwatching days in the 1950s, when every bird was new and I was constantly referring to my *Observers Book of Birds*.

Almost the first birds we saw in the park were a pair of Figbirds, so different in appearance that I was convinced we were watching two species! Blue-faced Honeyeaters and Black-faced Cuckoo-shrikes were duly sorted out by referral to the excellent Slater Field Guide, and then we were entranced by our first Superb Fairy-wrens, birds that we never tired of seeing. The dam in the middle of the park hosted a breeding colony of Australian White Ibis, while the water itself provided our first taste of Australian wildfowl, in the shape of Wood Ducks, Hardheads and the attractive Pacific Black Ducks. The surrounding lawns created an ideal habitat for our first Willy-wagtails, while Magpie-larks sought crumbs under the picnic tables. By the end of our first day we had identified 26 species, of which 25 were lifers. Not a bad start!

Superb Fairy-wren.

So on to the rainforest reserve of O'Reilly's, where we had three magical days being entertained by the Satin & Regent Bowerbirds, Green Catbirds and Logrunners, not to mention a whole host of beautiful, brightly-coloured parrots and rosellas, as well as a plethora of well-camouflaged 'little brown jobs' or 'LBJ's as they are known in England. Our personal highlights were not one but three sightings of Noisy Pittas, well seen and photographed in the low branches only a few yards away, having caught our attention by their persistent and haunting 'walk to work' song, while on our last morning we were able to track down four Albert's Lyrebirds.

Noisy Pitta.

The next four days were spent driving south to Orange, visiting several of the National Parks en route. Each day brought fresh challenges to our bird identification skills, as we attempted to sort out the myriad members of the honeyeater family, rather easier, however, than the infamous European *Phylloscopus* warblers. Our favourite location was Girraween NP, where we spent a most enjoyable day wandering around the rocky scrub and forest. Here we were able to enjoy the attractive Yellow-tufted Honeyeaters and found our first Shining Bronze-cuckoo and Yellow-rumped Thorntails. The highlight, however, was a majestic Little Eagle that soared effortlessly overhead and became our 100th species of the trip. On the following day, two chance stops along the roadside produced our first 'gang' of Apostlebirds, the only Red-capped Robin (a female carrying food) we were to see, as well as an agitated male Emu that had become separated by roadside fences from its charge of three well-grown juveniles.

And so we arrived at Orange to join the members of the CBOC on their annual weekend away. Immediately, we were made to feel part of the Club's extended family and for the next three days we explored the immediate neighbourhood around the town with our new-found friends. Our personal highlights were the magnificent Superb Parrots that were even present at the campsite, a pair of nesting White-throated Gerygones, and Musk Duck and Nankeen Night Heron at Lake Canobolas.

After leaving Orange, we spent a week visiting the birding hotspots around Sydney, particularly enjoying the company of Andrew Patrick as he showed us the nesting Brown & Grey Goshawks and Tawny Frogmouth on his home patch, not forgetting a roosting pair of Powerful Owls. Tony Dymond, John Durante and Keith Brandwood were all kind enough to take us out to other areas that we otherwise would not have found, enabling us to see Pink-eared Duck, Sharp-tailed Sandpiper (a real rarity in Britain), a pair of Spotted Quail-thrushes and the elusive Rock Warbler. Two of our favourite areas were Hawksbury and Pitt Town Lagoon, where we spent a most enjoyable second day taking in not only the birds but a game of baseball! A late afternoon spell on the marsh at Pitt Town

Lagoon was particularly rewarding with good views of Baillon's, Australian Spotted and Spotless Crakes!

A day around the shores of Botany Bay enabled us to catch up with some of the coastal waders that had so far eluded us. While familiar with Bar-tailed Godwit, Whimbrel and Grey Plover back home, the likes of Grey-tailed Tattler and Sooty & Australian Pied Oystercatchers added more species to our life lists, as did a single Eastern Curlew with its disproportionately long, decurved bill. A brief seawatch from a rocky headland produced, what would turn out to be, the only Australian Gannet and Wedge-tailed Shearwaters of the trip, albeit several miles offshore.

With just a week left we drove south to spend some time in the Royal National Park, an area that we certainly would like to revisit again in the future. Despite the increasingly overcast skies we enjoyed renewing acquaintance with many of the rain forest specialities that we had first encountered at O'Reilly's, while adding New Holland Honeyeaters to our ever-growing bird list. By mid-afternoon it was raining heavily and we returned to our hotel in Heathcote. The rain persisted throughout the night and for all of the next day, preventing us from venturing outdoors. However, we were able to enjoy the excellent set of DVDs produced by the CBOC, entitled *Let's Go Birdwatching*, presented so professionally by Andrew Patrick. It was also fun trying to pick out the CBOC members that we had met during the previous week. Unfortunately it was still raining intermittently over the following two days, limiting our exploration of the Royal National Park.

With just a couple of days left, we continued south spending a most rewarding morning on the shores of Lake Illawarra, where despite threatening skies the rain held off and surprisingly we were able to obtain some of the best bird photographs of the trip. We were also rewarded with 10 delightful Red-capped Dotterels on the sandy beach, as well close views of an adult and juvenile Australian Hobby, which turned out to be the final addition to our Australian bird list.

Red-capped Dotterel.

And so to Wollongong from where I was sailing (or so I thought) on one of the regular SOSSA pelagics to record and ring seabirds up to 40 miles offshore. After a restless night at the Boat Harbour Motel, dreaming of albatrosses and shearwaters, I awoke early and made my way to the quayside for the 7am start. Heavy overnight rain had persisted and was now accompanied by a force 6-7 gale. The omens were not good. Lindsay Smith, the leader of the trip duly arrived and unfortunately announced that it was unsafe to sail in view of a predicted 3 metre swell. The dozen or so hopeful seabird enthusiasts were understandably disappointed, none more so than Dick Newell, a friend from England, who had driven down from Sydney that morning, and of course me. Cruelly by mid-morning the wind had abated and glorious sunshine bathed the picturesque harbour in the afternoon. So ended our holiday in Australia with a final tally of 209 species, of which over half had been photographed well enough to be shown in future presentations.

Despite the last week of the trip, we both had had an unforgettable time, thanks to the superb birding and warm welcome extended to us by every single Aussie we had met, none more so than the members of the CBOC. Will we be returning? You bet we will!

Robina on the quayside at Wollongong.

This chapter finishes as it started with an account of a visit to Africa, this time to one of my favourite parts: southern Africa. The excerpts have been taken from one of several 'trip reports' that I have penned for the magazine *Birdwatch* and was entitled 'Escape to Africa':

Despite having visited South Africa on two previous occasions, I had yet to explore the avian delights of KwaZulu-Natal and the Kruger National Park, in the north-east of the country. While November may be the most popular time of year to visit this part of Africa, a mid-winter trip in January has many attractions, not least the chance to escape the British winter.

So it was that my partner and I arranged a private visit through the birding tour company Cheepers! Africa with my old friend Errol de Beer as our guide. Errol is one of the leading birding and naturalist guides in sub-Saharan Africa and during the three weeks that we enjoyed his company, his knowledge, skill and patience were always in evidence. Not only was he able to find over 400 species of birds for us, but we also managed to obtain photographs of over half, while the game viewing and photographic opportunities in the Kruger and other national parks provided ample scope for watching many of Africa's larger mammals.

After an overnight flight from London, we arrived in Johannesburg the following morning and from there we took a short internal flight to Durban, where we met up with Errol in mid-afternoon. It was marvellous to be greeted by blue skies and temperatures in the 30s, having left a cold and grey Norfolk the day before.

We were soon settling in to our accommodation for the next three nights at the Gateway Country Lodge at Umhlanga Rocks. The lodge is conveniently situated only a short drive from Umhlanga Lagoon Nature Reserve, a small wetland area with some coastal thickets, where we found our only Black-throated Wattle-eye of the trip. This species also provided an excellent example of the problems resulting from the change in names of many of the South African species, as it was called Wattle-eyed Flycatcher on my last visit in 2010.

The Reserve also hosts a large breeding colony of Eastern Golden and Thick-billed Weavers, which soon dived for cover when a juvenile Black Sparrowhawk flew low over the reeds.

Eastern Golden Weaver.

Nearby was the Umhlanga sewage works, a popular haunt of many birders, where we spent a most enjoyable morning watching the local wildfowl, including Red-billed and Hottentot Teal, and finding a rarity for South Africa in the shape of a Green Sandpiper, feeding with its commoner congener, Wood Sandpiper.

We spent a day at Benvie Farm, renowned for the large variety of birds in its 30-acre garden, including the very localised Orange Ground Thrush and the magnificent Knysna Turaco. On the journey we also found a colour-ringed White Stork that we subsequently learnt had been ringed in Croatia. The next three nights were spent at Kingfisher Lodge in St Lucia, where Hippos roam through the garden at night! It is situated near the iSimangaliso Wetlands Park, where the highlights included Rudd's and Yellow-breasted Apalis, Trumpeter

Hornbill and Purple-crested Turaco, while a colony of several hundred breeding pairs of Little Swifts under a road bridge provided a real photographic challenge as they wheeled around only yards away from us.

For me one of the delights of birding in sub-Saharan Africa is to find some of our summer visitors in their wintering areas, and the Park turned up trumps when a Corncrake flushed from the side of the road giving us excellent flight views. One of the range-restricted target species in the Park is Lemon-breasted Canary, and we were eventually rewarded with some excellent views as one fed with some of its commoner cousins, Yellow-fronted Canaries.

The Park is also home to a variety of larger mammals and here we had our first sightings of Common Waterbuck, Nyala, African Buffalo and White Rhino. Before leaving Kingfisher Lodge we had a last, early morning walk along the adjacent Gwala-Gwala trail and were rewarded with four more excellent species: Livingstone's Turaco, Green Malkoha, Woodward's Batis and best of all, a diminutive Buff-spotted Flufftail that scampered across the trail, looking for all the world like a newly-hatched chick!

After a fairly long drive we arrived at the Nibela Lake Lodge, a beautifully appointed lodge set in magnificent sand forest surroundings, the veranda of our room overlooking the shores of Lake Nibela. Wisely, Errol had opted to use the services of one of the local Zulu guides, Lucky by name and lucky by nature, as it turned out, for he was superb at finding most of our target species. He was also a delightful man and it was an added bonus to learn about many of the Zulu customs. His father having had no fewer than eight wives, Lucky was one of 69 siblings!

One of Lucky's first finds was a pair of roosting African Wood Owls in trees near the lodge's boardwalk, while out on the barren floodplain he quickly located an adult and juvenile Rosy-throated Longclaw, perhaps the most attractive of the three species of longclaw that we recorded on the trip. This savannah-like area also held the only 2 Buffy Pipits we saw.

Errol de Beer, Lucky and Robina on the Nibela flood plain.

I've always had a fondness for cisticolas, in fact on a previous trip to Tanzania my companions renamed them 'Taylor's testiculars', and I have always been amazed at Errol's ability to instantly identify these classic 'LBJs'. I now realise that they are very habitat-specific and there are only one or two species in any particular habitat, which considerably narrows the field. But Errol really excelled himself on this trip identifying no less than 11, including Pale-crowned Cisticola on the Nibela floodplain. Other notable species in the nearby forest included the difficult to find Eastern Nicator and Pink-throated Twinspot, and perhaps my favourite bird of the trip, a pair of Narina Trogons.

Wakkerstroom, on the Highveld plateau was the next stop on our tailor-made itinerary, an area of rolling hills and upland grass supporting a totally different avifauna. On the first morning here we easily found the endemic Yellow-breasted Pipit and a supporting cast of Sentinel Rock Thrush, Eastern Long-billed Lark and Buff-streaked Chat. A pleasant change from peering into the canopy of tall trees! Once again another local guide aided us in locating two very localised birds, Botha's and Rudd's Larks.

At another stakeout we were rewarded with good views of three more target birds: Barratt's Warbler, Bush Blackcap and in flight the tiny Black-rumped Buttonquail. On our last morning at Wetlands Country House, a Red-throated Wryneck graced the lawns of the lodge, seeking ants; it was a species that I was particularly keen to see.

It was now time to head into Swaziland, where some of my partner's family were living. Errol had booked us into the Silverstone Falls Lodge, just on the outskirts of Mbabane. It was an ideal place for birders to stay surrounded by mountains and with a fast-flowing river running through the grounds, along which Pied, Malachite, Half-collared and Giant Kingfishers were all seen during our two-day stay.

Red-throated Wryneck.

We visited Mlilwane and Malalotja Game Reserves while in Swaziland, the latter in the opinion of Errol being one of the most scenic parks in Southern Africa, as well as being one of the best places to see Blue Swallow. Once again herds of grazing antelopes were in evidence, including both Blesbok and Black Wildebeest accompanied by their calves.

Our third and final week had arrived and we were very much looking forward to our four-night stay in the Kruger National Park. The brainchild of Paul Kruger, the Sabie Game Reserve was established in 1898, from which the present Kruger National Park has developed, which covers 20,000 square kms. For several reasons we stayed all four nights in Skukuza Camp, the main administrative centre, although on reflection it would probably have been better to have stayed at two or three of the six rest camps that are scattered around the Park.

This outstanding National Park is absolutely fantastic for both birds and mammals. Although January is not the optimum time for game viewing in the Kruger, as the bush is lush, the dense grasses are tall and animals are not dependant on waterholes, nevertheless we still enjoyed some great mammal viewing and the birding was phenomenal.

We entered the Park at the Malelane Gate and the drive to Berg-en-Dal rest camp was perhaps the most exciting two hours of our stay – birds were everywhere and some of the highlights were Common Scimitarbill, Brown-headed Parrot and Cuckoo Finch, a species that is never easy to find.

The afternoon drive north to Skukuza rest camp will long be remembered for the variety of large raptors, in particular a Lesser Spotted Eagle with its characteristic 'drain pipe trousers', that was perched in a roadside tree. We also saw our first Lions, two young males only a few yards away, which we were able to watch from the safety of our vehicle.

Among many other highlights in the Kruger was a very confiding Allen's Gallinule at Biyamiti Weir, a female African Finfoot swimming downstream on the River Sabie and who could fail to be impressed by the beautiful Southern Carmine Bee-eaters. While the special mammal memories include a pride of 14 lions crossing a shallow river and a large herd of browsing African Elephants watched from the balcony of our lodge at Skukuza.

Southern Carmine Bee-eater.

Our return journey to Johannesburg took us via Mount Sheba and Dullstroom, where we successfully located some Gurney's Sugarbirds feeding on the flowering proteas.

Our final day's birding was spent at Bronkhorstspruit Dam Nature Reserve, which turned out to be most rewarding and enjoyable with superb photographic opportunities. Several races of Yellow Wagtail were busily feeding in the grassland amongst the Black Wildebeest; along the water's edge fed a flock of 60 Lesser Flamingos and several African Spoonbills, while a Black Heron entertained us with his umbrella-like wings while fishing in the shallows.

Lesser Flamingos.

A fine selection of waders along the muddy fringe of the dam included Kittlitz's and Three-banded Plovers, and 10 Marsh Sandpipers, but best of all was a small party of Black-winged Pratincoles that allowed very close approach. Feeding in the shallows were 15 Whiskered Terns, in various plumages and 2-3 White-winged Black Terns. Here as in many other areas, we were also treated to flocks of the beautiful Amur Falcon, surely one of the most attractive of the world's raptors.

All in all, a perfect ending to a magnificent holiday in this magical part of Southern Africa.

*   *   *

Chapter 9

Adventures on the high seas

View from the stern of the *Black Watch*.

Although my late wife, Fran, enjoyed foreign holidays, she really disliked flying, in particular all the associated waiting around at airports, but once we were in the air, she was a lot happier. So perhaps it was not surprising that in July 2002 we took our first cruise, on the *Black Watch* sailing to Norway and Spitsbergen, our first visit to Scandinavia and the Arctic Circle. This was to be the first of eight cruises on which I sailed, often as one of the lecturers, either with Fran or after she had died with my partner, Robina Churchyard. These trips enabled me to see many parts of Norway and South America that I might not otherwise have had the opportunity to visit. At the time of the first three cruises, I was one of the In the Countryside columnists for the *Eastern Daily Press* and so our adventures on the high seas provided interesting copy for my columns and the following accounts are extracts from some of these articles:

> ...After embarking at Dover, we sailed up the North Sea for 36 hours before reaching the south-western coast of Norway. Living as we do on the north Norfolk coast, we are only too aware of the storms that can occur in the North Sea, so we were pleasantly surprised to find that, at least on this occasion, the water was a smooth as a mill pond.
>
> As we sailed north, small parties of Kittiwakes passed across the ship's bows or temporarily followed in our wake. A few Gannets flew alongside, giving everyone on board excellent, close views of their handsome black-and-white plumage. The adults also displayed the delicate yellowish buff wash on their head and hind necks. All the trawlers that we passed had their attendant Herring Gulls, while a loose party of over 100 Fulmars were feeding around the shallower waters of one of the North Sea banks.
>
> With no land visible in any direction, and none likely for many hours, it seemed surprising to come across the occasional adult

Guillemot, accompanied by a youngster less than half its size. These young Guillemots drop off the breeding ledges about a fortnight after hatching and remain dependant on an adult for several weeks, drifting around in the sea wherever the current takes them.

By our third morning we were sailing along the Atlantic coast of Norway, which is long and unique, with its myriad of skerries, islands and fjords, some cutting inland for well over 100 miles. The first we entered was Sognefjord, along which we sailed for 60 miles before docking at Balestrand. Although the peaks lining the fjord were covered in cloud, the scenery was magnificent, and we could readily appreciate why cruises along the Norwegian coast are so popular…

…At both Balestrand and Alesund, we felt at home, with Greenfinches and Chaffinches present in the gardens, and mixed parties of Blue, Great and Coal Tits calling in the nearby woodland. However, extremely tame Hooded Crows foraging in the centre of Alesund brought us back to reality, as did an Eider, with a brood of young ducklings in tow, in the harbour.

Another day of cruising north and we had crossed the Arctic Circle, to dock in Tromso. This, the fifth largest Norwegian town, boasts the most northerly university in the world. While it was pleasantly warm on the day of our visit, the winter months are far less appealing. Indeed, the sun does not rise between mid-November and the end of January. In July, however, we were in the land of the midnight sun, and it literally remained daylight throughout the 24 hours.

A walk in the mixed birch and coniferous woodland above Tromso proved rewarding. The commonest birds were Willow Tits, far greyer on the back than those found in Britain and therefore easily separated from Marsh Tits. A high pitched 'tseep' betrayed the presence of a Redwing, no doubt a breeding bird, while a party of five Waxwings that flew over trilling, may well also have been local breeders, although they are apparently rare in this part of Norway.

Willow Tit at Tromso, Norway.

Our most northerly port of call was Honningsvag, the nearest town to the North Cape. From the nearby village of Gjesvaer, a small fishing boat took some of us out to the offshore island of Storstappen, home to a huge seabird colony. A keen northerly wind blew across the sound as we sailed over the choppy waters and a sudden burst of spray from the bows showered us with icy cold water. At last we fully appreciated that we were well inside the Arctic Circle!

Slowly we approached the island of Storstappen, its steep cliffs rising vertically out of the grey waters of the Arctic Ocean. As we came closer to the vast stack, towering many 100s of feet above us, we were all amazed by the sheer numbers of birds present. The sea boiled with 1000s of Puffins, initially bouncing like corks on the restless sea, then as we drew closer, taking off in droves and skimming low over the surface in flocks of 100 or more. Others would suddenly bob to the surface near the boat, having been fishing deep underwater as we approached.

At the base of the cliffs, groups of Shags stood around on the lower boulders, surveying the scene as if taking in the general melee in the water around them. Higher up the cliffs, a few Black Guillemots and Razorbills were dotted around, and higher still, on a series of horizontal ledges, stood Guillemots in serried rows. From here to the top of the cliff, perched precariously on the multitude of small ledges, were scattered colonies of Kittiwakes. Their constant cries almost drowning out the sound of the crashing waves on the rocks below.

Rounding a headland, we came across a large slab of rock, 100 feet or so above the water line, on which were nesting over a 1000 pairs of tightly packed Gannets. Grey, downy young were clearly visible on some of the nests, while non-breeding, immature birds were sat around the periphery of the colony. Gazing upwards beyond the top of the island, we realised that the air was filled with yet 1000s more puffins, wheeling around above the scree slopes on which they breed. But best of all, the island held a pair of breeding Sea Eagles. An adult and several immatures were playing on the updrafts and these enormous raptors even dwarfed the nearby ravens. This was a truly magnificent sight.

Norway had done us proud and we still had the delights of Spitsbergen to look forward to:

Spitsbergen, or Svalbard, is an archipelago that lies in the Arctic Ocean midway between Norway and the North Pole. It consists of seven principle islands, which appeared in early Norwegian folklore, and were rediscovered by a Dutch expedition under the command of the navigator William Barents in 1596.

The Norwegians began coal mining on Spitsbergen in the 1890s, and the islands were used as the starting point of several polar expeditions, including that of Roald Amundsen, who is commemorated with statues in several of the towns we visited. Whilst the scenery in Norway is impressive, that in Spitsbergen is truly spectacular. Vast glaciers, the snow and ice reaching right down to the edge of the Arctic Ocean, separate the dark, foreboding mountains, whose peaks are enshrouded with mist. Much of the ice takes on a blue, or even pink, hue as a result of minute bubbles of air trapped inside. The air was clean and crisp, almost certainly the most unpolluted that any of us had ever breathed. But most memorable of all was the wildlife.

Wherever we looked 100s of Little Auks were skimming low over the surface of the water, with whirring wing beats, in lines or loose groups of up to about 30 birds. Some making their way to the offshore feeding grounds, others with full crops streaming back to their nesting holes under the scree on the coastal and inland mountainsides…

…We stopped at three ports of call in Spitsbergen, the first being Longyearbyen. To call it a town is an overstatement. A few wooden buildings line the only 'street' that leads inland to the glaciers and snow-crowned peaks. A derelict coal mine, long since abandoned, adds further to the impression of a ghost town. It was here that we came across our first Snow Buntings, the males resplendent in their black and white breeding plumage. One was accompanied by a recently fledged youngster, whose identity would have tested me to the limit had it not been with its parent. Uniformly grey with just the barest suggestion of some white in the wing, it gave no hint as to its true identity. It was also here that we had our closest views of reindeers. Although Fran and I had planned to walk to the edge of the nearest glacier, we were warned not to leave the settlement for fear of encountering a polar bear. This warning was reinforced when we saw that all groups of walkers leaving the area were accompanied by someone carrying a high power rifle!

If we had thought that Longyearbyen was desolate, we were all in for a shock when we docked at Barentsburg, a Russian mining settlement on the west coast of Spitsbergen. Fran described it as the most depressing place that she had ever visited, and we all felt truly sorry for the small Russian population that worked there on two-year contracts. Goodness only knows what the conditions must have been like back home in Russia, if they would rather live in Barentsburg!

The jetty at Barentsberg was barely long enough for our cruise ship to dock alongside, but eventually we were made fast and those wishing to go ashore disembarked. A huge pile of rusting waste metal at the dock and run-down wooden huts were a far cry from the luxuries on board. While most of the passengers climbed a long series of steps that led up to the main settlement, my attention had been attracted by two pairs of Glaucous Gulls that were nesting on a grassy slope above the harbour…

…Our final port of call, and what was to turn out to be the most interesting, was Ny Alesund, an environmental research centre. Here the collection of well maintained wooden buildings surrounded by the Arctic tundra was a delight to the eye. On disembarking, it was readily apparent that the settlement also acted as an attraction to the Arctic birds, which showed very little fear of Man. Arctic Terns were nesting by the side of the main tracks that meandered between the buildings, and woe betide anyone who dared to wander too near a nest! The incubating bird would be up in an instant, making repeated dives at the miscreant's head.

Groups of Barnacle Geese grazed fearlessly on the lusher areas of vegetation, many accompanied by their young goslings. But the most exciting find was a magnificent adult Ivory Gull, typically very tame, that was feeding near a huskies' pen. Being a full adult, it displayed pure white plumage, unlike the immature at Aldeburgh in 1999. A family of silvery-grey Arctic foxes had set up home under one of the buildings and we were all enthralled to watch them running around and feeding less than 50 yards away.

But for everyone on board, including the crew, the highlight of our cruise was the discovery of a female polar bear accompanied by two well-grown cubs, slowly ambling across a scree slope, as we sailed into one of the smaller fjords. A truly memorable climax to our journey to the land of the midnight sun.

Our next cruise was on *Discovery* and saw us sailing around Britain and Ireland in late August 2003, setting sail from Harwich:

The weather was perfect, with clear blue skies and only a light breeze to ruffle the surface of the sea as we headed north around the Suffolk coast, passing familiar landmarks such as Landguard Point and Sizewell. But all too soon the sun had begun to set and it was time to leave the deck to go below for our evening meal.

As the next day was to be our only one entirely at sea, I was up at dawn in the hope of seeing a good selection of seabirds as we sailed up the North Sea to our first port of call, Kirkwall, in Orkney. As on last year's cruise, I was constantly being reminded of the vastness of this expanse of open sea, with no land in sight and only the occasional trawler visible on the horizon. Shortly after going up on deck, the familiar thin 'tseep' of a Meadow Pipit caught my attention, and there it was flying across the stern, steadfastly sticking to its south-westerly bearing as it headed towards the English coast still many miles away. Seeing such a small bird in this alien environment certainly brought home the marvels of migration.

Occasional Fulmars glided across the smooth water created by the ship's wake, but I was quite unprepared for a gathering of several 1000 that peppered the surface of the sea as we passed near the Dogger Bank. Presumably they were attracted by food brought up from the shallower water…

…One of the birds that I particularly wanted to see was the Storm Petrel, a diminutive sea bird, barely larger than a swallow. It was the only British breeding species that I had not previously seen. Storm Petrels nest on inaccessible rocky islands and coasts around northern Scotland and the Irish Sea, but fly into their nesting burrows only under cover of darkness. Daylight hours are spent miles out to sea feeding and resting. Therefore as we sailed further north I spent more and more time scanning the surface of the sea in my attempt to find one of these elusive birds.

At last my patience was rewarded and I spotted not one, but two, flying low over the waves about 100 yards off the stern. Very similar in size and shape to a House Martin, the similarity even extending to the upperparts, which are all black with a white rump patch. However, the white rump was more extensive than on a martin, wrapping around onto the rear flanks. After over 50 years of birdwatching I had at last added Storm Petrel to my life list! Having seen one, of course, I then had no difficulty in picking up small groups of them on several of the other evening seawatches, but none compared with that first, long-awaited sighting…

…The next morning found us sailing into Cobh, formerly known as Queenstown, at the entrance to the second largest natural harbour in Europe, which leads up to the city of Cork. Cobh is an attractive and fascinating town, steeped in maritime history, and we thoroughly enjoyed hearing about its colourful past from our Irish guide, as we wandered around the narrow cobbled streets. Many thousands of Irish men and women left from here to build a new life in America, especially during the famine years in the mid nineteenth century.

Cobh was also the last port of call for the Titanic on her fateful maiden voyage. It was strangely moving to see the old wooden landing stage from where the passengers boarded the ferry that took them out to the Titanic, moored just outside the entrance to the harbour. It was while standing there and pondering the fate of those Irish emigrants that I noticed a small, distinctly marked gull flying alongside the harbour wall – an adult Sabine's Gull, a rare visitor from the High Arctic, an ironic coincidence in view of the fact that an iceberg was responsible for the sinking of the Titanic just over 90 years ago…

…As luck would have it, I failed to wake up early on the following morning, and by the time that I got up on deck we were only a few miles off St Mary's, the largest of the Isles of Scilly. Overnight rain, the first that we had encountered on the cruise, had clearly caused a small "fall" of migrants. A Wheatear was flitting around the ship's railings and more surprisingly a very tired and tame Dunlin was probing the grooves between the boards of the stern deck for any possible morsels, while the open-sided restaurant on the top deck hosted another Wheatear and half-a-dozen exhausted Willow Warblers.

Once at anchor, local boats from the island began ferrying the ship's passengers across the choppy water to the small harbour at Hugh Town. Having previously visited Scilly on a number of occasions, I had already planned to cover as much of the southern part of St Mary's as possible in the limited time available. Heading out of Hugh Town, I was soon in Old Town Bay, admiring the magnificent view past Gull Rock towards the wide open Atlantic Ocean, the waves crashing down on the rocky headlands around the bay. A few Greenshanks and a Common Sandpiper were feeding along the water's edge of the sandy beach, along with the local gulls and Oystercatchers. Continuing on along the narrow, windy roads I was soon on the Higher Moors nature trail leading down to Porthellic Pool. A scattering of

Pied Flycatchers and Willow Warblers in the sallows were a sure sign that an overnight "fall" had occurred, but all too soon I had to return to the ship, for our final night at sea.

Over the next few years, further invites followed to join ships as a cruise lecturer to Iceland and The Baltic, but my favourite destinations were always the Caribbean and South America. The following article appeared in *Birdwatch* in January 2015:

> While many birders will think of cruises as being the domain of old folk, who enjoy over-eating, being entertained and generally being lazy, if carefully selected, a cruise can be a most enjoyable way of visiting parts of the world that otherwise might not be easily accessible. It's certainly true that some of the cruises I have been on have resembled floating residential homes, but this hasn't detracted from the pleasures of days at sea and the birding opportunities in the ports of call.

Enjoying the sun on *Black Watch*.

> Personally, I prefer cruises that do not involve a flight, but depart from and return to the same English port. This avoids all the inevitable aggravation at airports, and means that within a short time of arriving at your port of departure, you are on board, and ready to set sail. For birders it also has the great advantage that there are no worries about excess baggage. The only restrictions are - will it all fit into your cabin? So tripods, telescopes, long lenses and field guides can all be packed, along with suitable clothing for any type of weather, with no concerns about the weight.
>
> From a birding point of view, the smaller cruise ships (carrying 7-800 passengers) are far better than the massive, more modern ships that take several thousand passengers and resemble floating hotels. On

the smaller ships, there are several decks from which to watch out for seabirds and, in general, the lower the deck the better. Cruises in the Northern Hemisphere are best taken in spring and summer, while the longer winter cruises south of the Equator not only provide winter sunshine, but also the opportunity to visit some of the best birding places in the World.

Without doubt, my favourites have always been those to South America, even though they have involved a five to six day Atlantic crossing each way, which during the winter months can be surprisingly birdless. On occasions, in mid-Atlantic a whole day can easily pass without a single bird being reported. Most trans-Atlantic cruises sail south through the Bay of Biscay, before berthing for day stops at, for instance, Madeira, Tenerife and Mindelo, each of which has its own avian attractions. On Madeira, Trocaz Pigeon and Madeiran Firecrest are the main species of interest, while Tenerife is the home to Laurel's and Bolle's Pigeons, Berthelot's Pipit and the recently split African Blue Tit. Although the islands' pigeons are largely confined to the less accessible laurel forests, at least on Tenerife the target passerines are readily found within walking distance of the harbour at Santa Cruz.

My favourite island, however, is Sao Vicente in the Cape Verde islands, where the port of Mindelo is only a short taxi ride from the town's sewage works, located near the oil storage depot, clearly visible as one sails into Mindelo. In fact we enjoy going there so much that I have taken Robina there twice as her birthday treat!

Robina birdwatching at Mindelo sewage works on her birthday.

With its extensive old-fashioned type of filter beds, it provides ideal conditions for passage waders, as well as vagrants from across the Atlantic. On each of my three visits to Mindelo, Black-winged Stilts and Kentish Plovers were not exactly unexpected, but I was delighted to find up to 5 Lesser Yellowlegs on each occasion and on one memorable day, both Greater Yellowlegs and Blue-winged Teal as well.

At this point, a word of warning about the organized excursions from the ship. Don't be tempted into taking them. Almost without exception, they can be arranged privately far more cheaply on the quayside, by taking local taxis or even buses. Not only that but you can choose exactly where to go and how long to stay ashore. Almost inevitably, other birders will also be on the cruise, and by far the best plan is to make up a party of six to eight and take a taxi or minibus to suitable locations within driving distance of the harbour.

As stated earlier, the Atlantic crossing is often a time simply for reading and enjoying the warm weather, but there is always the chance of shearwaters and petrels, especially in the south Atlantic or Pacific Oceans, as well as cetaceans, such as Humpback, Sperm and Killer Whales, and several species of dolphin. Once in the western Atlantic, and especially as the ship approaches the Caribbean, floating masses of seaweed from the Sargasso Sea in which the elvers destined for European rivers become more noticeable, along with flying fish and the first Red-billed Tropicbirds, Magnificent Frigatebirds and Masked Boobies.

Most cruises will call in at one or more of the Caribbean islands, each of which has its own fascinating avifauna, often only a short distance away from the port. Some islands do not have a harbour sufficiently large to take a cruise ship and passengers are ferried ashore in the ship's lifeboats. These smaller islands are often the best for birds, such as Grand Turk, where two salinas just a short walk from the landing jetty act as magnets to overwintering North American waders. On one memorable occasion a Stilt Sandpiper posed with a Black-necked Stilt and Lesser Yellowlegs, creating an unforgettable threesome. While the Auberge Seraphine in Castries, St Lucia hosts an egretry around a pond in front of the hotel and provides unrivalled photo opportunities.

Black-necked Stilt, Lesser Yellowlegs and Stilt Sandpiper on Grand Turk.

But of all the cruises I have been on, two to South America stand out in my memory, but for totally different reasons. The first, a three-month cruise on Fred Olsen's *Balmoral* in 2012, included in its itinerary four Caribbean islands, three southern states in North America, four Central American countries and five in South America. Of all the places we visited our favourite was Chile, from the point of view of the birds, the welcome extended to us by the locals and the general safety we felt during our excursions into the more remote areas.

Of the many raptors we saw in Chile, the Chimango Caracara was the most widespread (after the ubiquitous Turkey and Black Vultures), a species that has an amazing ability to change its outline in flight to take on the appearance of an accipiter one moment, then a harrier and even a falcon!

Chimango Caracara in Chile.

While the weather in Chile was generally warm and sunny, it became much colder the further south we sailed. However, this did mean that Black-browed Albatrosses became far more numerous, along with five other species of albatross. After entering the Beagle Channel we sailed around Tierra del Fuego on an atypical calm day with the sea more like a mill pond!

Black-browed Albatross in the Beagle Channel.

Our next port of call was Stanley in East Falkland, where a one-day stay simply whetted the appetite for the wildlife delights of this unique outpost of the United Kingdom. While it is possible to hire a private taxi on East Falkland, none were available at the time of our visit and we had no choice but to take one of the organized tours, which in the event proved to be an excellent introduction to the birds of the Falklands. The highlights of the three-mile walk around a reserve to the west of Port Stanley included Magellanic Penguins, Buff-necked Ibis, Falkland Flightless Steamer Ducks, Upland and Kelp Geese, and Black-throated Finch.

After leaving the Falklands we sailed north to Uruguay, before continuing along the Brazilian coast to Rio de Janeiro, where we took a taxi across the city to the Rio Botanical Gardens which turned out to be excellent for birds, especially hummingbirds, such as Reddish Hermit, Violet-capped Woodnymph and Sombre Hummingbird, which certainly lived up to its name! The final part of our South American odyssey involved sailing up the Amazon as far as Santarem, a bird-rich journey that warrants an article on its own, but suffice it to say that it provides an excellent introduction to the wildlife of Amazonia. By the time we had returned to Southampton, my personal bird list for the trip stood at over 450, in addition to six species of whales and five dolphins. A truly memorable cruise.

White-throated Hummingbird in Uruguay.

The second unforgettable cruise was in 2014 on board the *Marco Polo*, again a cruise to the Amazon, but this time sailing 1,000 miles up river as far as Manaus. However, from beginning to end it was a litany of disasters and warrants a chapter on its own.

*　*　*

Chapter 10

The ill-fated cruise of the Marco Polo

The *Marco Polo* moored in port.

It all started in late September 2013 with a Readers' Offer in one of the Sunday papers, offering a very reasonably priced cruise on the *Marco Polo* to the Amazon, a destination that Robina and I had visited two years earlier. In fact the offer seemed too good to be true, and that's exactly how it turned out! So it was that on 5th January 2014 we boarded the *Marco Polo*, which was to become our 'home' for the next six weeks. During our embarkation at Tilbury Docks we mingled with passengers that were disembarking from the previous cruise, who warned us that the weather in the North Sea was pretty stormy, which was not the sort of news that we wished to hear. In fact, as we pulled away from the pier at Tilbury, the ship was blown back by the gale force winds on to the dock, which splintered the wooden deck, causing the stevedores to leap back from the bollards around which the ship's mooring lines had been tied. A rather inauspicious start to our cruise, but nothing compared with what was to come. We subsequently learnt that as we sailed up the Thames one of the portholes in a passenger's cabin had been blown in!

The bad weather continued as we crossed the North Sea and after a day of sightseeing in Amsterdam we sailed south stopping at Lisbon and Madeira, before continuing on to Sao Vicente, one of the Cape Verde Islands. This was our third visit to the island and once again we headed for the Mindelo sewage works, which acts as a magnet for American waders, as well as those migrating between Europe and Africa. In fact it's so famous it's actually featured in a mural on the harbour wall!

Mural of Mindelo sewage works on harbour wall.

Once again it did not disappoint with both Greater and Lesser Yellowlegs present on the filter beds.

Greater Yellowlegs at Mindelo sewage works.

But the *Marco Polo* jinx struck again as we were about to cast-off from the harbour at Mindelo. Fortunately everyone had embarked when the concrete supporting a lamp-post on the harbour wall suddenly collapsed, fracturing an oil pipe that contained the diesel for refuelling the cruise ships. The men on the dock ran around like headless chickens looking for the stop cock and it was eventually turned off, but not before a large quantity of diesel had escaped and had begun to flow into the sea. If the passengers had been boarding at that moment, the outcome might well have been far more serious.

Fractured diesel pipe at Mindelo harbour.

So began our four-day crossing of the Atlantic in fine, sunny weather with calm seas, but very little in the way of birdlife. However, we were able to enjoy the company of other passengers, some of whom were also keen birders, such as Martin Latham from Oxford, Dave Williams from Wales and Jerry Bart from East Dereham in Norfolk.

Martin, Dave, Robina & Jerry.

Once we had passed Macapa at the mouth of the Amazon, and started to sail upriver towards our first port of call, Santarem, we began to encounter an interesting selection of South American birds on the river banks, over the water or in the forest, such as White-faced Whistling Duck, Capped Heron, Large-billed Tern and Scarlet Macaw.

Large-billed Tern.

One of the non-avian delights of sailing up the Amazon is the wonderful variety of brightly-coloured moths that are attracted at night by the ship's lights, and which try to hide away on deck at dawn.

Atlas moth on deck.

As a result, as soon as we had moored at the dock at Santarem, some South American flycatchers flew aboard and perched on the ship's rails to seek out this ready supply of food, none more attractive than the Fork-tailed Flycatcher. While Great Kiskadees waited on the wooden posts on the pier, occasionally making sallies to catch moths that had been disturbed by the disembarking passengers.

Fork-tailed Flycatcher.

Santarem is very much isolated in the middle of the Amazonian rain forest and so, apart from flying in, the river itself forms the only route for entering and leaving the city, and boats take the place of local buses. One of the highlights of a day at Santarem, is a boat trip to Lake Maica, an oxbow lake on one of the small tributaries of the Amazon. The journey itself is fascinating, passing the riverside homes built on stilts to avoid flooding as the river level fluctuates. It also provides an opportunity to witness at first hand the locals going about their daily lives, who are clearly living on the bread line. An interesting variety of birds is always seen from the boat and on the trip this year we recorded both Savannah and Roadside Hawks, as well as the ubiquitous Great Egrets.

Great Egret.

Once back on board the *Marco Polo* we continued sailing up the Amazon as far as Manaus, from where we were able to take another boat trip, this time to January Island, where we encountered Three-toed Sloths, as well as several species of kingfisher and woodpecker.

Three-toed Sloth.

While most of us simply took back to the ship photographs of the wildlife we had encountered, such as a Guira Cuckoo with its punk hairdo, and pleasant memories of our short stay at Manaus, four passengers who had eaten in one of the dockside cafes, brought the norovirus back on board, which resulted in most of the ship's amenities being closed for the next three weeks! Two other passengers were robbed in the town, one lady losing a gold necklace and the other £250 from his back pocket, but it was their own fault as they had been warned not to carry any valuables ashore.

Guira Cuckoo.

Six days later, after sailing down river to the mouth of the Amazon and then north around the Brazilian coast, we arrived at Ile Royale, one of the three islands that comprise the Iles du Salut, off the coast of French Guiana. Translated into English, the name of the group means the Islands of Salvation, so named because missionaries went there from the mainland to escape the plague. However, the name was hardly appropriate in the mid-19th century when they were used to imprison the most dangerous criminals deported to the French Penal Colony along the border between French and Dutch Guiana. Escape was considered impossible because of the shark-infested waters around the islands.

Main prison block on Ile Royale

Just across the water from Ile Royale lay Ile du Diable, Devil's Island, which was used to house political prisoners and it was here that Dreyfus was imprisoned for four years at the end of the 19th century after his conviction for treason. It was also here that Henri Charriere was imprisoned for 14 years after he was wrongly convicted of murder (according to him!), as he described in his semi-autobiographical novel *Papillon*, the nickname by which he was known. The book was turned into a film starring Steve McQueen and Dustin Hoffman, in which Papillon escapes by leaping from a high cliff with two floats of bagged up coconuts. He'd noted earlier that every seventh wave that came into the small harbour on the island, rebounded from the rocks and would be powerful enough to carry him out to sea. But high cliffs don't exist on Ile du Diable and in fact the film was largely shot elsewhere. However, Charriere did manage to escape by sea and reach the mainland, eventually arriving in

Venezuela, where he became a national hero and was granted citizenship. The penal colony was finally closed in 1953 and Charriere continued to live in Venezuela at least until 1973, when he published a sequel to *Papillon* entitled *Banco*.

Ile du Diable from where Charriere escaped.

Ile Royale turned out to be one of the most interesting, and certainly moving, excursions on the cruise. When a cruise ship is unable to moor in a reasonably-sized harbour, passengers are transferred ashore on the ship's tenders or lifeboats, and this was the case at Ile Royale. We were fortunate in being able to get tickets for the second transfer, as those passengers on the later ones had far less time to explore the island. As we walked around the prison block it was clear that life must have been very harsh for the inmates, and many were guillotined for minor offences, as was depicted on a contemporary painting in the prison chapel. Prison warders also lived on the island with their families, and the presence of a font in the chapel and children's graves in the cemetery were an indication that babies were born here but some succumbed to tropical diseases in their childhood.

Painting in the prison chapel of an execution.

Apart from a few French soldiers caring for this 'tourist attraction' the only other mammalian residents on the island now are Brown Capuchin monkeys (the monkeys of organ grinders) Squirrel Monkeys (popular as pets in South America) and Agoutis, large rat-like ground mammals, which were very approachable and fearless.

96

Brown Capuchin on Ile Royale.

Amongst the birds that we came across were several species of tanagers, Scarlet Macaws and the Neo-tropical bird family with my favourite name: Common and Spotted Tody-flycatchers.

Pair of Scarlet Macaws.

All too soon it was time for us to return to the small wooden pier to board the tenders for our return to the *Marco Polo*, but even this was not without incident. A large swell on the sea caused the tenders (the ship's lifeboats in the event of the ship being abandoned) to repeatedly strike the side of the *Marco Polo* and bounce back as the passengers were disembarking. This resulted in two of the lifeboats being damaged and holed, but fortunately above the water line! It clearly was a fated cruise.

One of the ship's lifeboats used as a tender.

At least the four days spent sailing around the Caribbean and visiting Grenada, St Vincent, St Lucia and Barbados were uneventful and we were able to add nearly 30 species to our trip list, including a drake and two female Masked Ducks on Barbados, one of only nine lifers that I recorded on the cruise.

Drake Masked Duck on Barbados.

From the West Indies we sailed back east across the Atlantic and as we approached the Azores, on the fifth day, the Captain of the *Marco Polo* warned us that the weather was rapidly deteriorating and we should expect rough seas ahead. Little did we know at the time, how rough it was to become! In the event we spent two very pleasant days sight-seeing on Sao Miguel, visiting the Scrimshaw Museum above Peter's Café, and the hot springs, where we were surprised to find three feral cats laying on the warm ground around the springs, despite being soaked from the heavy rain. Who says that cats don't like to be bathed?

Three bedraggled cat at the hot springs on San Miguel.

Birds, of course, were not neglected and we were delighted to find amongst the Azorean Yellow-legged Gulls at Ponta Delgada harbour, three Glaucous Gulls and one Iceland Gull, both species being rarities in the Azores. Undoubtedly their presence was due to the northerly gales that we were to encounter on leaving the island.

Second-winter Glaucous Gull with Azorean Yellow-legged Gulls.

So we set sail for home in the late afternoon of February 11th, the day on which the norovirus restrictions on the ship were at last lifted. Within a day or so, the weather had deteriorated and we were being pounded by gale force winds and big seas. By February 14th, Valentine's Day, we were in the middle of a storm the like of which many of us on board had never before encountered. In fact one of the guests on our dining table had been an engineer in the Royal Navy for 25 years and he later told us that he had never experienced such strong winds and mountainous seas.

From dawn on that day, all decks were closed except for the quarterdeck but with winds blowing at storm force 10, gusting to violent storm force 11 and 30-foot waves crashing over the deck, I quickly retreated inside. Robina and I went to the Bistro for our breakfast and were eating our cereal, when the ship suddenly lurched sending the plates, cups and glasses slithering across the table and tipping my chair sideways flinging me to my feet. Still clutching my plate, I pirouetted across the Bistro, and ended up against the wall, still holding my plate and its contents! The Bistro was subsequently closed and all meals had to be taken in the ship's main dining room on one of the upper decks.

View from the quarterdeck on the morning of February 14th.

During the morning, most people remained in their cabins as the storm continued unabated and the ship rolled violently from side to side. Lunchtime arrived and on reaching the Waldorf Restaurant we were directed to the last vacant table on the port side, next to one of the large picture windows, through which we could see the angry seas. Thereafter passengers began to fill up the starboard side of the dining room, commencing with the tables by the windows. Despite being on one of the upper decks, occasional waves were even crashing over the glass of the windows, especially on the starboard side, from where the gale-force winds were coming. The waiters were really struggling with the trays and dishes, attempting to keep hold of them while at the same time trying to stay on their feet. A loud crash from the kitchen indicated that plates were being thrown on to the floor by the violent lurching of the ship.

View through the window on the 7th deck on February 14th.

Suddenly there was a loud gasp from the passengers on the starboard side as an enormous wave broke over a window on that side of the dining room, followed a few moments later by a crashing sound as the same window caved in through the pressure of the next wave. A moment's silence was broken by screams, as the enormity of the situation became apparent to those sitting near the smashed window as seawater began to pour into the dining room through the hole left by the missing glass, as the ship was struck by a series of giant waves. Amazingly there was no real panic and following instructions from the head waiter, we all began to exit the Waldorf Restaurant in an orderly, if rather frightened, fashion, wading through water several inches deep that now covered the floor, as it slopped around with the rolling of the ship. Robina and I looked back at the table we had vacated and were amazed to see our two dining companions still sitting and eating their lunch. When we saw them later and asked why they hadn't joined us and left the restaurant, the wife said that the fish she was eating was the only tasty dish they had eaten all cruise and she was damned if she was going to waste it!

In the struggle to get out of the restaurant several people fell over and injured themselves, while others suffered cuts from the broken glass. We subsequently learnt that a second window had also been blown in and had flown across the dining area like a flying saucer, but thankfully had landed harmlessly on the floor in the middle of the room. Less fortunate had been a man sitting at the table by the broken window, who had been struck on the head by the broken glass and subsequently died of his injuries. How lucky Robina and I had been, for if we had arrived at the restaurant a minute or two later, we might well have been sitting at that table.

For the remainder of that day and night, we were all confined to our cabins for our own safety, with food being delivered by our cabin steward, Marko, who couldn't have been kinder and more reassuring, for like many passengers on board, we feared that the ship might founder. The storm continued unabated throughout the night, during which the injured passengers were airlifted from the ship by helicopter, thanks to the bravery of the pilot and his winch man.

Much to everyone's relief, we arrived safely at Tilbury docks two days later, to be met by a barrage of television crews and newspaper reporters waiting as we disembarked from the ship. Robina and I had no hesitation in telling them of our experiences and as a result appeared on several television channels and made the headlines in our local papers. Needless to say, we have not been on any more cruises!

LUCKY: Dr Moss Taylor and his partner Robina Churchyard reflecting on their cruise on the Marco Polo where a pensioner died in raging seas.
Main picture: ANTONY KELLY

Cruise ship couple talk of storm seas tragedy

Headlines in the North Norfolk News on 20th February 2014 (*Antony Kelly*).

*　*　*

Chapter 11

Through my study window

The garden of my home, Cherrymead, in summer 2015.

Gardens are becoming an increasingly important habitat, particularly in winter, and perhaps surprisingly especially in rural areas. The latter point has become more apparent to me in recent years, while carrying out fieldwork for the BTO and Norfolk Bird Atlases, as well as surveys for the North East Norfolk Bird Club. Arable fields and their surrounding hedgerows (if they still have any) are often devoid of birds, until one passes a country cottage or enters a village, when the number and variety of birds noticeably increases. To many people, watching birds in their gardens is often their only contact with nature, and the enjoyment that they obtain is reflected in the thriving trade in bird food products. Despite spending many thousands of hours each year in the wonderful Norfolk countryside, I still obtain enormous pleasure from studying the birds visiting my garden. The following accounts of the more exciting records were first published in the North East Norfolk Bird Club's monthly newsletter, *The Pied Flyer*:

> Just over 46 years ago, on 4th August 1972, I moved into my present house, Cherrymead, in Sheringham, where I have lived ever since. Although it had a well-established, mature garden of about a quarter of an acre, which had originally been part of an orchard, over the years many additional trees and shrubs have been planted around a central lawn. Over time all of the original apple trees died and there are now

no fruit trees, which used to attract thrushes and Blackbirds to the fallen apples. Tall poplars also lined the southern border of the garden but these too had to be felled due to honey fungus. In their place some maple saplings were planted and developed into fine mature trees, but only one remains as the rest were damaged by an extensive fire in a neighbour's garden that unfortunately spread into mine. Without doubt the tree that is most attractive to birds is a beautiful silver birch that I planted many years ago as an unwanted sapling from Hickling Broad, where the Norfolk Wildlife Trust was trying to control their spread. More recently I also planted about 20 sallows to create a small wooded area as a net site for catching birds for ringing.

Mist net in sallows with Siskins and a Brambling caught for ringing in spring 2011.

Finally a small pond at the end of the garden also proved an attractive proposition to many birds. However, many of the species have only been added to my garden list as a result of a small balcony that I had built on to the back of the chalet bungalow, from which I can look over the town, the golf course and Beeston Bump to the north, and the Cromer to Holt Ridge to the south.

The author looking south from his balcony in 2014 (*Chris Taylor*).

During the years I have lived here, 151 species of birds have been recorded in, over or from the garden, although this does include three that are known to have been escapes (White Stork, Crested Caracara and Cockatiel). Perhaps the most surprising are the number of waders (19 species), but the vast majority of these were simply flying over and were identified, at least initially, from their calls, such as the plovers, godwits, sandpipers and shanks, and many of these were recorded from the balcony.

Woodcock on snow-covered lawn at Cherrymead in March 2018.

No fewer than 19 species have been recorded less frequently in recent years, some of which have shown a national decline in numbers over the same period, such as Turtle Dove, Cuckoo, Lesser Spotted Woodpecker, House Martin, Song Thrush, Spotted Flycatcher, Marsh and Willow Tits, Starling, House and Tree Sparrows, Greenfinch and Bullfinch. Of these it is worth mentioning in particular the Starling and House Sparrow. During the 1970s Starlings were daily winter visitors to the garden in large numbers, with over 100 present together on many occasions, particularly in hard weather. They then became fairly scarce and far less frequent during the 1990s, while today the presence of one or two Starlings in the garden is a rare occurrence! However, a never-to-be-forgotten sight occurred in the late afternoon of 3rd November 2006, when an enormous flock estimated to contain about 1,500 Starlings suddenly descended on the back lawn, forming a complete black carpet, and they remained busily probing the grass for about five minutes before taking off en masse and flying to the west, presumably to a roost. I arrived at the estimated count by calculating the average distance between each bird and multiplying this by the area of the lawn.

Similarly, the House Sparrow was a common and almost daily visitor to the garden in the 1970s and 1980s but became far less numerous during the 1990s, although they were still present almost daily throughout most of the year in 2000 and 2001. Since then numbers have fallen dramatically and two pairs on the feeders on 23rd

February 2016 were the only ones recorded in the garden that year, and none have been seen since!

On the plus side, however, there are 18 species that I now record more often in or over the garden than during the first 20 years of living here. Prior to 1994, I had recorded Pink-footed Geese on only three occasions, whereas since then large skeins are recorded annually flying over between their roost sites in west Norfolk and feeding areas in the south-east of the county, with a maximum of 3,000 in October 2004. A similar marked increase in the number of records since the mid-1990s has occurred with Cormorants, Sparrowhawks, Mediterranean Gulls, Magpies and Bramblings. While since the introduction of the smaller black sunflower seeds and sunflower hearts in the 2000/01 winter, many Goldfinches have largely changed their migratory habit of overwintering in Iberia and instead remain in Britain throughout the year, with a resulting increase in the numbers visiting garden feeders in winter, including mine.

Adult male Sparrowhawk from study window in March 2016.

Barely a year goes by without one or two scarce or rare birds turning up in the garden. Within a month of moving to our house in Sheringham my wife, Fran, rang me in the surgery to say that a Wryneck was feeding on the patio outside the lounge window. As soon as the patient I was with had left, I drove straight home and fortunately the Wryneck was still there greedily devouring ants on the paving slabs. It turned out to be the first of four that graced our garden in the next four years, but sadly none since. The following year I was amazed and delighted to see a Great Grey Shrike on November 1st sitting on the hawthorn hedge eyeing up a Blue Tit that was caught in a nearby mist net. I hasten to add that the Blue Tit came to no harm!

Adult male Black Redstart in garden in April 2011.

I well remember the early evening of 12th June 1983 when 2 Spoonbills flew west over the garden and caused a temporary halt to the game of badminton that I was playing with my sons. This was in the days when Spoonbills were far less common and it was almost exactly 30 years later on 13th June 2013 that the only other two to fly over the garden were recorded. On 3rd May 1990, the first real rarity, a Serin, flew over calling on two occasions but could not be subsequently relocated. Without doubt the bird that attracted most attention from visiting birders was a female Rustic Bunting that first appeared on my lawn on 27th April 1996 and stayed for the next five days, during which time it was admired by several hundred visitors. Its appearance coincided with a one-day BTO conference that I had organised at UEA, and amongst the speakers were Ian (DIM) Wallace and David Parkin, both of whom were staying with me. Needless to say Ian was up at the crack of dawn on the day after the conference and enjoyed prolonged views as the bird fed on the mixed wild bird seed that I had scattered on the grass.

Painting of Rustic Bunting by Ian Wallace.

[On returning home Ian very kindly sent me a collage, painted by him, of the more interesting species that we had seen over the weekend, including the Rustic Bunting, as well as Glaucous Gull, Garganey, and the first Wheatear and Sandwich Terns of the spring, all at Weybourne, accompanied by the following letter.]

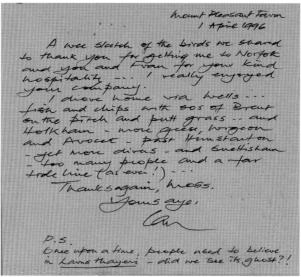

Letter from Ian Wallace that accompanied his painting.

In September 2001 a Yellow-browed Warbler announced its presence in the poplars at the end of the garden with its characteristic call, but it stayed only briefly, as did another one in the autumn five years later. A fine male Firecrest discovered in one of my mist nets in November 2003 was a very pleasant surprise, as was a female in the front garden on 15th March 2019.

Female Firecrest in front garden in March 2019.

Early morning watches from my balcony, with the first cup of coffee of the day, were well rewarded on 26th April 2006 when a

Purple Heron flew west, having drawn attention to itself with its distinctly different call from that of a Grey Heron. Three years later, the balcony produced another new species for the garden list when a Richard's Pipit flew west calling stridently in late September. While screaming Common Swifts are seen flying daily over the garden and town during the summer months, a Pallid Swift flying around Beeston Bump on 27th October 2011 was visible through a telescope set up on the balcony and the following August an Alpine Swift, also flying around Beeston Bump, was added to my garden list, courtesy of the balcony.

I could scarcely believe my eyes on 1st September 2014 when I realised that the rather chunky finch clinging on to a bird feeder on the crab apple tree was a juvenile Common Rosefinch. It even remained long enough for me to get my camera from the car and take a couple of shots from the lounge. No my eyes had not been deceiving me!

First-winter Common Rosefinch in September 2014.

Perhaps the most unlikely addition to my garden list was a Long-eared Owl being mobbed by Magpies, Blackbirds and tits in one of the maples at the end of the garden in the early morning of 18th October 2015. Shortly after being spotted it flew off to the east and was subsequently found later in the morning on Beeston Common, where I managed to catch up with it again! Thanks to a pager message, I added Great White Egret when one flew over the town and Beeston Bump on 16th October 2017. The final addition to date was a male Hawfinch by a feeder in early April 2018, no doubt part of the unusual influx the previous autumn.

Hawfinch in April 2018.

A second article described the highs and lows of ringing almost 22,000 birds in the garden between 1972 and 2015, and highlighted some of the more interesting movements, as shown by the 346 recoveries reported to date:

> For most of my birding life, ringing has been a major area of interest leading on to my fascination with the wonders of migration, so on moving to my present house in Sheringham in 1972, I quickly established several mist net sites around the garden, some of which were still in use, when I stopped ringing in 2015. Between 1972 and 2015, I ringed just under 22,000 birds in my garden, of which the grand total for five species exceeded 2,000: Blackbird (2,001), Blue Tit (2,244), Starling (3,705), Siskin (3,627) and Greenfinch (4,837). Not surprisingly this number of birds produced some impressive recoveries, while over the years I also controlled a good number of birds ringed elsewhere in Britain, as well as in other parts of Europe.

> In the early years, one of the most successful methods of catching the birds was by using an elastic-powered clap net. Attached to a pole at either end, which pivoted, the 60-foot net was laid on the lawn and was thrown over the catching area by the action of the stretched elastic. Like the old fashioned sieve and a stick, it was also operated by pulling a string leading from one of the poles to my lounge window. Primitive it may have been, but it was still highly effective and over the years accounted for 3,700 Starlings, over 600 gulls and a Kestrel. The only downside was all the kitchen scraps that were used to bait the area and attract down the birds, food which I used to obtain from raiding the pig bins at the local nursing homes. I have little doubt that I was also keeping alive a healthy, or should I say unhealthy, population of rats.

Starlings feeding in area of clap net in January 1976.

> January 1976 was particularly memorable, not only for the severe weather and heavy snow across Europe, but also for the number of Starlings coming to my feeding bonanza on the lawn and, in turn, getting caught. During the month 450 Starlings were ringed and subsequent recoveries indicated from where the influx had originated: two in Finland and two in the USSR, including one found dead four months later at Ukhta, which is situated almost as far east as the Ural mountains, and one of the most easterly recoveries of a British-ringed Starling. The other birds that were attracted to the food on the lawn in

winter were gulls, especially Black-headed Gulls, and over the years 562 were ringed in the garden, resulting in 33 foreign recoveries: 19 in Fennoscandia, 10 in western Europe and two in the Baltic States, while seven foreign-ringed gulls were also caught.

Winter was also the time that thrushes and finches were attracted to the garden by fallen apples, holly berries, peanuts and sunflower seeds. A cold snap in January 1985 that happened to coincide with a particularly heavy crop of holly berries on the tree in my front garden enabled me to ring record numbers of Fieldfares (30), Redwings (42) and Mistle Thrushes (8). While the opening months of 1987 were characterised by the large numbers of Greenfinches visiting my garden feeders and by the end of the year no less than 885 had been ringed, showing just how much the population of this species has declined in recent years.

Back in 1963, the first Siskins were recorded feeding in Surrey gardens and from there the habit spread to neighbouring counties and eventually to many parts of England, including Norfolk. Initially it seemed that shelled peanuts in red plastic bags were necessary to attract them but soon they were coming to any type of nut feeder and I ringed my first Siskins in the garden in 1984. Although the number varied from winter to winter, Siskins soon became regular visitors to my garden feeders and proved extremely easy to catch in increasing numbers. It was only through ringing that I quickly realised just how many different individuals were involved, as shown by the totals of 579 ringed in 1994, 398 in 2006 and a grand total of 3,627 over the 44 years. Siskins have also produced the most recoveries from my garden birds, as many other ringers in the British Isles are also trapping them in their gardens, with the result that the 32 exchanges of ringed Siskins between my garden and Scotland clearly indicate that this is a major area from which many of our wintering Siskins originate.

Adult male Siskin caught for ringing in March 2011.

While Siskins may have increased in recent years, some species have entirely disappeared as garden visitors and this is reflected in the annual ringing totals: no Marsh Tits have been ringed since the five up to 1974, although oddly enough more Willow Tits were ringed (11) but again none since 1983. Surprisingly few warblers have been ringed, apart from the two winter visitors: Blackcap (35) and Chiffchaff (14). However, I have probably had more than my fair share of unusual and rare birds turning up in the nets: Lesser Spotted Woodpecker (2), Firecrest, Pied Flycatcher (7), Black Redstart, Grey Wagtail and Rustic Bunting. Nowadays I simply enjoy watching the birds in my garden, and no doubt they are delighted to be able to go about their business undisturbed!

Male Lesser Spotted Woodpecker caught for ringing in October 1985.

*   *   *

Chapter 12

Books and my foray into publishing

For as long as I can remember, I have enjoyed reading and collecting books. As I explained at the start of the first chapter, it may well have been the two books entitled *The Billy Beaver Book* and *Peter the Puffin*, which I received as prizes in the late 1940s, that stimulated my interest in natural history. As a young teenager, I always used to say that Christmas was incomplete without a book as one of my presents, and almost invariably it would be a bird book, and strangely enough I still feel the same over 60 years later.

However, it wasn't until I moved to Sheringham in 1972 that I first developed my obsession with collecting bird books, after seeing Alan Haven's extensive library in his home at Weybourne. Since then I have become addicted to perusing second-hand bookshops and charity shops, and buying a large number of new books on birds as they are published. My current library contains over 1,500 books on birds and other aspects of the wider natural world. Although it is mainly used as a reference library, I also enjoy reading autobiographies and travelogues, as well as books on Norfolk and those written by the early East Anglian naturalists, such as Arthur Patterson.

Again, as I explained in an earlier chapter, it was through attending a lecture given by Percy Trett at the Great Yarmouth Naturalists' Society that I was introduced to the writings of 'John Knowlittle' or Arthur Patterson, the famous Yarmouth naturalist. He wrote no fewer than 33 books and pamphlets between 1884 and 1930 about his experiences in Broadland, especially around Breydon Water. I soon became an avid collector of his fascinating books, fortunately before they became as collectable and expensive as they are nowadays.

While playing golf at Sheringham many years ago, I discovered that my golfing companion was none other than the great grandson of my hero, Arthur Patterson! My game immediately deteriorated even further. From his father, Steve Hales had inherited a fine collection of books by Arthur Patterson, some of which were duplicates, and he kindly offered to sell these to me at a very generous price. Imagine how delighted I was when I discovered that some had been gifts to other members of his family, and *Notes of an East Coast Naturalist* had not only been personalised but he had also included a pen-and-ink sketch of a Grey Heron.

Inscription in *Notes of an East Coast Naturalist*.

While another, *Man and Nature on the Broads*, one of his earliest books and published in 1895, is inscribed "To Maud Paston with Uncle Arthur the authors Kind Regards. Jan 20 1925" (His wife's maiden name was Paston). When scanning the shelves of second-hand bookshops, I am especially attracted to books that have previously belonged to well-known ornithologists, and such was the case with another Patterson classic *Nature in Eastern Norfolk*, which I purchased many years ago. The spine indicated that it had once been part of a library collection and on the inside cover was the bookplate of the Cavendish Library at Eastbourne College in Sussex, along with the signature of E.C.Arnold, the headmaster. Arnold was a renowned bird collector (shooting the first English specimen of Arctic Warbler on Blakeney Point on 4th September 1922, which is now in the Castle Museum, Norwich), naturalist and author in the early years of the 20th century. He was largely responsible for igniting an interest in the natural world in one of his pupils, Richard Fitter, who himself went on to become one of the century's outstanding naturalists. Arnold's memory is commemorated in the name of Arnold's Marsh at Cley, in Norfolk, and so here was an interesting additional local connection.

Library plate and signature in *Nature in Eastern Norfolk*.

My first copy of one of Norfolk's classic county avifaunas, *A History of the Birds of Norfolk* by B.B.Riviere, albeit with a slightly damaged spine, has on the inside cover the bookplate of David Armitage Bannerman, one of the most prolific authors of bird books during the middle years of the 1900s. He is best remembered for his 12 volume classic *The Birds of the British Isles*. Of particular interest was that this copy of Riviere's book was given to Bannerman as a present on his 57th birthday on 27th November 1943, possibly by one of his relatives, as judged by the inscription in the front of the book. My second copy of Riviere's avifauna is in much better condition and even has a reasonable dust jacket. It too has a fascinating hand-written inscription inside the front cover: "To my friend Capt H.A.Gilbert who ruined my pike fishing on the Norfolk Broads by introducing me to the Wye Salmon. March 31st 1939. From Jim Vincent, Hickling, Norfolk". Here was another of Norfolk's renowned ornithologists, who worked as the head keeper of the White Slea Estate at Hickling in the first half of the 19th century. In 1911, Vincent kept a diary in four volumes, which were published as a single book in 1980, by his son Edwin Vincent, under the title *A Season of Birds*.

In 1912, a seminal book on the British avifauna was published under the title *A Hand-List of British Birds*, in which the British and foreign distribution of each species was described. It was the forerunner of the *Practical Handbook* and later the five volume *The Handbook of British Birds*. Between each page of text was inserted a blank page on which personal notes and sightings could be written. I was lucky enough to obtain a copy of *A Hand-List of British Birds* but it was only later that I realised that scattered throughout the book on the blank pages were hand-written notes on sightings made in the Hickling area dated between 1894 and 1929. The neat writing in pen-and-ink was very distinctive and was identical to the inscription in the front of Riviere's book mentioned above. So this book had belonged to none other than Jim Vincent and included many of his personal sightings made from the age of about 10 into his 40s, before and during the time that he was the keeper on the Hickling Estate.

This period was the time when most of the eminent naturalists were also collectors, and would think nothing of shooting a rare bird to confirm its identity or to offer it for sale as a specimen. In this respect Jim Vincent was no exception, as was clearly demonstrated in his copy of *A Hand-List*. Under Water Pipit he writes: "March 20th 1911. Shot one for identification purpose and sold to E.Connop for £5. It was running about on a bank of weeds pulled out from edge of Deep Dyke with 3 Rock Pipits", while under Bluethroat he states: "May 16th 1906. Shot a beautiful adult male after heavy rain at Hickling". However, on occasions he resisted the temptation to collect a rare bird as he recounts for a Cream-coloured Courser: "June 13th 1913. Saw a bird of this species which stayed for 2 days. It frequented some dried mud-flats near White Slea, and I watched it for hours, only 25 yards away". It obviously was well within range of his gun. On other occasions, Vincent's entries are amusing and show that 'What's hit is history and what's missed is mystery' is not always the case, as with an entry made in 1914 under Red-breasted Goose: "Nearly 18 years ago during a severe winter my father shot a small goose which I feel certain, after knowing more of birds, was an immature of this species. I saw the [bird] myself and told my father at the time it was a rare goose, though I was only 13 years of age, but it was foolishly eaten"!

Jim Vincent did not confine his exploits to Hickling but made several visits to Cley on the north Norfolk coast. One visit in late September 1908 was especially memorable when he saw a Yellow-browed Warbler on the 25th "...at Cley next-Sea amongst the bushes, and saw 2 that had been shot the previous day here", while under Red-breasted Flycatcher for the 23rd he wrote: "When at Cley, Norfolk, saw a perfect specimen of this species brought in to Mr Pashley the taxidermist here."

Nash Pashley was born at Holt in 1843 and died in 1925 aged 81. Although he had had a lifelong interest in birds and practiced taxidermy as a hobby, it wasn't until he was over 40 that he set up as a professional taxidermist. He worked and lived in his little shop in Cley village from c.1884, where he remained for the rest of his life. He had been persuaded to do this by two keen collectors, Drs Frederick & George Power, both London physicians, who regularly visited the Cley and Blakeney area to obtain specimens. They were the first of the 'Gentleman Gunners' to give Pashley regular work in preparing birds for their collection. Pashley's fame as a taxidermist soon spread and he was never short of work. His house and shop are still in the High Street in Cley, but are now divided into two houses: Pashley's House & Georgian Cottage.

From 1887 to 1924 Pashley kept a diary of the more interesting specimens that passed through his hands, and these were included in his book *Notes on the Birds of Cley, Norfolk*. Sadly it was not published until a few months after his death in 1925. It is now a very valuable and collectable book. One amusing entry following the famous Pallas's Sandgrouse invasion of 1888 reads: "All the Sand-Grouse taken at Cley and the immediate neighbourhood were taken from June 1st to October 17th. The Protection Act came into force on February 1st 1889, after the birds had all left. I had 33 specimens through my hands, the highest number throughout the Kingdom for any one taxidermist. 'Not that that is anything to your credit,' says Mr J.H.Gurney. I did not shoot one of them, so no need for Mr J.H.G. to make such a remark."

My own copy of Pashley's book has passed through the hands of several notable birdwatchers, as shown by the book plates and signatures inside the front cover. Initially owned by Peggy Meiklejohn, nee Barclay, who was given it as a present in the year of publication 1925. She then passed it on to Richard Richardson and it ended up in David Musson's collection in 1998 from whom I bought it when his books were auctioned at Keys in Aylsham to raise funds for the BTO.

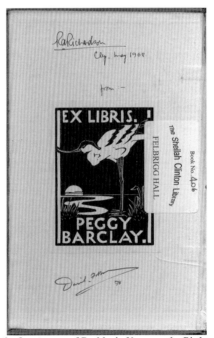

Inside the front cover of Pashley's *Notes on the Birds of Cley*.

Mention has been made earlier of Richard Richardson and his service during the Second World War in India. When I was collecting together material and stories prior to writing his biography, I was sent a very worn copy of Salim Ali's *The Book of Indian Birds* published by the Bombay Natural History Society in July 1944, in which some of the black-and-white photos had been coloured in with paint. But of great interest inside the front cover was written 5781627 R.A.Richardson. Deolali, India. March 1945. Royal Norfolk Regiment, India Command. This had all been lightly crossed through and C.M.Thorburn's name had been added. Exactly who he was I have been unable to ascertain, but the surname of Thorburn is an extremely well-known one in the field of bird illustration. This had clearly been Richard's 'field guide' and reference book while he was stationed in India, but it would be fascinating to know why and how it went out of his possession. It now forms part of my important R.A.R. archive.

Salim Ali's *The Book of Indian Birds.*

Although I had already written or co-authored two books, published by Poppyland Publishing and Pica Press respectively, I decided to set up my own publishing company, Wren, for Richard Richardson's biography, for which I had started to gather material in 2000. However, as I quickly discovered there's a lot more to publishing one's own book than just writing it and getting it printed. This was where the talents of one of my son's came in very handy. Having obtained an honours degree in Graphic Design at the Norwich School of Art, Nik used his professional expertise to design the layout and gave invaluable advice prior to submitting the book to the printers, as well as designing the Wren logo. I decided to use Crowes Complete Print in Norwich and what a wise decision that was. One of the directors was Mike Dawson, a fellow birder, and without his help the book would never have seen the light of day. Since then I have used the same printers (although the name has changed to Swallowtail Print) for seven of the books that I have published under Wren Publishing, with Mike Dawson still at the helm.

Cover of *Guardian Spirit of the East Bank.*

As an author, one of the greatest thrills is to see your own book in print, and the elation does not diminish with subsequent publications. I really had no idea how many copies of *Guardian Spirit of the East Bank* to have printed but following advice from Mike, I opted for 1,500 bearing in mind that over 230 people had contacted me with stories and anecdotes about their friendship with Richard Richardson, and the number of pre-publication orders I had received. One thing that I was not prepared for was the vast number of boxes of books that Crowes delivered to my house. I just hadn't appreciated the space that 1,500 large format books would occupy! Many piles of boxes stood in our spare bedroom and my study, although eventually all were sold or otherwise distributed.

On 9th August 2002, the book was launched at an exhibition of Richard's artwork and other memorabilia, held at St Margaret's Parish Church, Cley to which all the contributors were invited. James McCallum kindly lent his display boards for hanging Richard's paintings, and the exhibits were arranged by Martin Woodcock. The church was full to capacity to hear Richard Fitter, with whom Richard Richardson had worked on *The Pocket Guide to British Birds* and *The Pocket Guide to Nests and Eggs*, and the well-known artist Robert Gillmor, speak about their long associations with RAR. A total of 73 original RAR watercolours were exhibited illustrating over 50 species of birds, the largest exhibition ever of Richard's artwork. The exhibition was open for two days and proceeds from the event were given to the church roof restoration fund. All profits from the book went to wildlife and conservation causes dear to Richard's heart.

The author, Richard Fitter and Robert Gillmor at the book launch (*anon*).

The following year I decided to publish a small booklet with a selection of one hundred of my *Eastern Daily Press* columns covering such diverse topics as bird migration, antifreeze in butterflies, why Robins feature on Christmas cards and accounts of many of my favourite haunts in East Anglia and abroad, as well as a small selection of my photographs taken on these wanderings. Again my son Nik was responsible for the layout of the book and Robert Gillmor very kindly agreed to design a suitable cover. Robert and I had first met as members of the Publicity and Membership Committee of the BTO, and had become good friends when he and his wife, Sue, had moved to Cley. I felt especially honoured as Robert had been designing the dust jackets for the *New Naturalist* series of books since 1985. For my book he produced a superb three-colour linocut entitled "Hunting Harrier, Norfolk". It captures perfectly the atmosphere of a wetland area in north Norfolk, and I was particularly pleased that he included it in his beautifully-produced book, *Cutting Away*, in which a large selection of his linocuts are illustrated. Rather ambitiously I ordered a print run of 750 copies of *In the Countryside*, and I still have one or two left although it was published 17 years ago! Here was a salutary lesson for all would-be authors, but from each book sold, I was pleased to make a donation to the *EDP* We Care Appeal.

Cover of *In the Countryside.*

Over the next few years, I was asked to publish several other bird books by Norfolk authors and agreed to undertake the necessary work on four: *The Birds of Blakeney Point* by Andy Stoddart and Steve Joyner, *Birds New to Norfolk* by Keith Dye, Mick Fiszer & Peter Allard (for which my son, Chris, took the excellent photos of mounted specimens at the Castle Museum, Norwich), *Echoes from Cape Clear* by Tom & Stephanie Green and *The Norfolk Cranes' Story* by John Buxton and Chris Durdin. Robert Gillmor again kindly agreed to design the covers of the first two. As with *In the Countryside* we were perhaps too optimistic about the number of copies printed of the first two (again 750), but the last one sold out and it was hoped that a reprint would be possible.

Wren Publishing books by other authors.

For my two most recent books *Wings over Weybourne* and *Rare and Scarce Birds in North-east Norfolk*, I chose a more realistic print run of 150, and I'm pleased to say that they both sold out within a couple of years. Writing in 1930, Arthur Patterson wrote "Very few nature writers get back the cost of their productions and the majority lose." While it is still true to say that the authors of bird books aren't in it to make money, it should at least be possible nowadays to recoup all the costs and even make a little profit. By self publishing, as I have done for my latest books, at least I have been able to donate just over £600 to Love for Leo, our fund-raising organisation that helps to finance equipment that is not otherwise available for children in Norfolk and Suffolk with cerebral palsy. Similarly, once the costs of this current book have been covered, all profit will be given to Love for Leo.

Fortunately the only book with which I have been associated that has been a complete flop was *Collins Identifying Birds by Colour* that was published in 2008. I was responsible for writing the introductory section and the species' texts, while Norman Arlott painted all the colour illustrations. By arranging the order of the birds according to their colour, it was felt that this would considerably help beginners to identify any birds they encountered. As far as we were aware this was a novel method. Unfortunately, another publishing house had the same idea and even the covers of the two books were very similar, and it didn't help that they were both published in the same year. Despite the fact that ours was translated into three other languages, sales even failed to cover our royalty payments!

*   *   *

Chapter 13

Rarities and reintroductions

Although I had seen a good selection of species abroad, which were rare or scarce visitors to Britain, the first one that I actually found for myself in England was a Bluethroat. As described in an earlier chapter, it had turned up in one of my mist nets at South Ockendon in Essex, during the spectacular fall of Scandinavian drift migrants in September 1965. This was followed the next autumn by a Richard's Pipit that Jimmy Flynn and I were lucky enough to find at Holliwell Point, on the Essex coast opposite Foulness Island, which itself was a hot spot for rarities. Surprisingly it was an addition to the county list. Naturally following my move to Norfolk in 1969, my opportunities for finding and seeing rarities increased dramatically, but I could never call myself a 'twitcher'.

However, over the years certain birds have turned up that I felt were justified in 'twitching', usually because they were species that I had not previously seen and were unlikely to turn up again in Norfolk. One of the first was the Little Whimbrel that was found at Blakeney Eye on 24th August 1985, only the second British record following one in Wales three years earlier. A Siberian breeding species, it is the smallest of the world's curlews and attracted hundreds of admiring birders during its ten-day stay in the Cley and Salthouse area. Later that year on 8th December, I succumbed to the temptation to 'twitch' my first North American passerine in Britain, a Black-and-white Warbler in the Broads at How Hill. Despite being one of the commonest and most widespread American wood warblers, it is a very rare visitor to these shores, and an unlikely addition to the Norfolk list. I was able to watch it down to about 15 yards as it fed in the manner of a Treecreeper in silver birches and an oak tree, while being admired by about 500 other 'twitchers'!

Black-and-white Warbler at How Hill in December 1985 (*Pete Morris*).

Another highly unlikely addition to the Norfolk list was the Red-breasted Nuthatch that graced the woods at Holkham in 1989. This was an even rarer bird than the Little Whimbrel, being a first for Britain & Ireland. Initially found near the Royal summer house (which was unfortunately burnt to the ground a few years later), it proved to be very elusive but once the identification had been confirmed and the news had been disseminated on the Birdline Information Service, an estimated 2,000 birders had assembled hoping to see this vagrant from North America. In the event, it remained in the Holkham and Wells pine woods until the following May, either delighting or frustrating an endless procession of birders, as it was so aptly put in the *Norfolk Bird Report.*

On occasions, trips to see rarities can be combined with other reasons for visiting more distant parts of Norfolk, as was the case in one of my In the Countryside columns appearing in the *Eastern Daily Press* in February 2002:

> Like my fellow columnists, my wife and I enjoy visiting arboreta, and often spend a day admiring the exotic trees in such collections during our holidays in England. But, the trees are not the only exotic species that can be found in such areas, as I discovered last week at Lynford Arboretum, where a rare Olive-backed Pipit had been present since early February.
>
> It really was a gem of a bird, performing beautifully to the assembled crowd of admiring birdwatchers during each day of its stay. To the non-aficionado it could easily have been passed off as a dull, boring "L B J" or "Little Brown Job", as it crept around amongst the dead leaves or through the long grass, constantly pumping its tail. But examined more carefully through a telescope, its distinctive head markings were clearly apparent: a broad white supercilium, the characteristic white "tear drop" behind the ear-coverts and bold black thrush-like markings on the breast. However, the most surprising thing about this record was that here was a summer migrant that by all accounts should have been wintering in India!

But it is considerably more satisfying to find one's own birds and on two occasions I have been fortunate enough to be in the right place at the right time when small flocks of birds that are unusual visitors to Britain have flown past. On 1st June 1998, I was standing with Mick Fiszer by the duck pond at Salthouse, when we picked up a flock of five herons flying in from the north-east and heading straight towards us. Imagine our surprise and delight when we realised that the flock consisted of four Purple and one Grey Heron! They circled over the village, then headed back north before returning over Salthouse and finally departing to the south-east. Rather surprisingly, they were not spotted at any other localities, but during the five minutes they were in sight, several other observers at Salthouse were also able to enjoy this once in a lifetime spectacle. On the second occasion I was playing golf at Sheringham on 14th October 2009 when a flock of eight Great White Egrets flew east-south-east above the cliffs and continued on inland. They had been seen at Cley a few minutes earlier and were subsequently seen at Mundesley, strangely enough by Mick Fiszer, who had seen the four Purple Herons with me at Salthouse. At the time this was the largest flock of Great White Egrets to have been recorded in Britain.

However, on occasions I have to admit to having been unable to resist the temptation to travel many miles to see a 'lifer', that is one that I had not previously encountered. But I think that I can honestly say that I have never gone further than Suffolk, in the pursuit of one bird, as I described in one of my In the Countryside columns in the *Eastern Daily Press* in December 1999:

> I don't chase after rare birds and so by definition I'm not a twitcher. But I was unable to resist making a trip to Aldeburgh in Suffolk in mid December to see an Ivory Gull that had turned up a few days earlier.

As this was the only species of gull to have been recorded in Britain that I had not seen before, I felt that my action was justified! Strangely enough, the last time that I had 'twitched' a bird outside Norfolk was also a gull in Suffolk - the Franklin's Gull from North America that overwintered in the Lowestoft area in 1977-78.

So, 20 years after last chasing a bird outside my home county, I found myself on a bitterly cold morning outside the White Lion Hotel at Aldeburgh. If I'd had more sense, I would have been inside warming the inner man. The conditions, of course, were perfect for the Ivory Gull, which is a resident of the High Arctic, usually staying near the pack ice throughout the year. In fact, it ranges further north than any other species of bird.

Here I was able to enjoy spectacular views of this attractive bird, at times down to about 20 feet. When on the ground it was remarkably pigeon-like, with a rounded body, short neck and short, black legs. Being a first-winter bird, its gleaming white plumage was flecked with a few fine black spots, as were the tips of the flight feathers and the tail, while blackish feathers around its face gave it an almost ruffian-like appearance.

Every couple of hours it fed greedily on codling which had been discarded around the fishermen's huts and boats, skilfully extracting the contents of the chest and abdominal cavities through a small hole below the gills. After gorging, it sat hunched up on the pebbles, fitfully dozing, while occasional drips could be seen collecting, and then falling, from the tip of its bill. In common with other seabirds, Ivory Gulls possess well-developed nasal glands which secrete a strong saline solution, thus maintaining normal salt levels in the blood and body tissues. It was this solution that could be seen dripping from the end of its bill.

As I suspected at the time, this is still the only Ivory Gull that I have seen in England, although I was lucky enough to watch an adult feeding in a husky pen on Spitsbergen three years later. A rather amusing sequel to the story of the Aldeburgh bird occurred a few days after I saw it, when it became entangled in fishermen's nets drying on the beach. It was rescued by Kevin Elsby, another Norfolk ringer, who had travelled to see it and who disentangled and released it, before realising that he had his bird rings in the boot of his car. Had he remembered, it would have become the first Ivory Gull to be ringed in Britain!

Back at home in Sheringham, there have been many rarities that I have enjoyed seeing, some of which have been described in an earlier chapter, but only a short distance from home, is Beeston Common, the location for a most obliging Isabelline Shrike in October 2015, an event worthy of inclusion in one of the local newsletters *Just Sheringham*:

For over a week, Beeston Common played host to an Isabelline Shrike, a rare visitor from Central Asia, that in turn attracted a steady stream of admiring birdwatchers from both near and far. Found initially by a visiting birder, who no doubt was looking for one of the Yellow-browed Warblers that Mark Clements had found during the previous week, the Isabelline Shrike remained faithful to a small area of scrub and bushes on the northern side of the common, where it avidly fed on wasps.

Isabelline Shrikes breed in Central Asia and winter in north-east and east Africa, and this individual was undoubtedly blown onto the north Norfolk coast by the strong north-easterly winds that had prevailed for several days.

The first Norfolk record of this rare species was one at Holkham in October 1975, since when only six more have been found in the county. However, amazingly two others were also located around the Norfolk coast this autumn, at Holkham and Mundesley, and on one day, October 15th, all three were present, the first time ever in Britain that three Isabelline Shrikes have been present in a single county on the same day.

Isabelline Shrike on Beeston Common in October 2015.

The circumstances surrounding rarities at Weybourne Camp that I have been lucky enough to find or see are included in the final chapter. I would to conclude this one with some personal thoughts on reintroductions, which are rather like Marmite, you either love them or hate them. But first a few words about Ruddy Ducks. It was in the late 1950s that a few escaped from Slimbridge, which led to a small viable feral population. The species first bred in the wild in Britain during the 1960s at Chew Valley Lake in Avon, and subsequently spread to the West Midlands and then further afield such that by the early 1990s the species was also breeding in Northern Ireland, Scotland and Wales. By the year 2000, the population was estimated to be around 6,000 birds. When Ruddy Ducks first appeared on the Continent and concern was expressed that they would hybridise with the closely related White-headed Ducks in Spain, an eradication programme was suggested in Britain & Ireland. I felt so strongly about this that I wrote an article, which was published in *Bird Watching* in August 2003 under the appropriate heading 'Hold fire!':

I live in Norfolk and here Ruddy Ducks are still relatively scarce. So, coming across one or a pair is always satisfying. The highly ritualistic bubbling display by the drake never fails to enthral and amuse, but it is not only for 'sentimental' reasons that I am strongly opposed to the culling of this introduced species. I am concerned about the reasoning behind the proposal and the simple practicalities of any such scheme.

The problem may well have arisen because of an unfortunate human error more than 50 years ago, when the species was first introduced to the wildfowl collection at Slimbridge, but this does not mean that we have to make a second mistake attempting to correct it.

Currently, six or possibly seven species of stifftails are recognised worldwide, three in the New World, including the Ruddy Duck, and three others endemic to the Old World, one each in Africa and Australia plus the White-headed Duck in Europe, Asia and North Africa. DNA analysis suggests that the first stifftails were found in tropical areas of South America, before spreading into the temperate zones of North and South America, and later still into Australia, Africa and Eurasia.

Although Ruddy Duck x White-headed Duck hybrids are fertile, this does not indicate that they are conspecific. Indeed, DNA analysis shows that they have been geographically isolated for several million years. However, the presence of Ruddy Ducks, believed to be from Britain, is felt by some to be threatening the very survival of White-headed Ducks as a separate species, through hybridisation.

There is no question that the world population of White-headed Ducks did decline from the 1960s onwards, but it now appears to be relatively stable, thanks to conservation measures taken worldwide. Surely the next step is to monitor the situation closely to detect any future changes in numbers, rather than embarking on a programme to eradicate the Ruddy Duck from the European avifauna.

In addition, according to the *Handbook of the Birds of the World*, the decline in recent years was caused by habitat loss, especially in Turkey, Russia and Pakistan, and excessive hunting disturbance in the wintering areas. Therefore a more appropriate solution for the survival of White-headed Ducks would be a network of reserves throughout its range, not the culling of another species more than 1,000 miles away!

What evidence is there that UK Ruddy Ducks are crossing the North Sea or English Channel in autumn? British Trust for Ornithology ringing data show that of about 350 Ruddy Ducks ringed in the UK, fewer than 4% have been recovered, the furthest less than 200km from the place of ringing, and no ringed birds have been recovered from abroad.

Wildfowl have one of the highest recovery rates for ringed birds, with the Mallard approaching 20%. It is therefore surprising that so few ringed Ruddy Ducks have been reported. If any carrying British rings had been shot in Spain, they surely would have been reported. There is also no evidence from observations of visible migration around the coast that Ruddy Ducks are regularly departing our shores. Despite a literature search, I have been unable to locate a single record of a Ruddy Duck having been observed during a seawatch.

To suggest, therefore, that the UK population is the source of annual records in Iceland and other gatherings in Europe is purely speculation.

Finally, what about the practicalities of a large scale cull? Already 2,600 Ruddy Ducks have been killed in the UK, and yet the population has apparently risen once again to more than 5,000. The difficulties of shooting the birds should not be underestimated. When danger threatens, their habit of diving, rather than taking flight, makes the task for marksmen even more difficult than is the case with most other species of wildfowl. The shooting of Ruddies puts other species at risk of being shot directly by mistake, as well as exposing some very sensitive wildlife sites to considerable disturbance.

DEFRA has estimated that it will cost up to £5.5 million to reduce the UK Ruddy Duck population to 175 birds within ten years. Will this come out of the taxpayers' pockets (the majority of whom I'd guess are against the cull) or will it be financed by the European Union?

Until such questions are answered, public anxieties about disturbance are dispelled and the true status of the migration of UK Ruddy Ducks and the effects of hybridisation are fully answered, we should not be seeking to eradicate this delightful newcomer to the UK avifauna.

In the event, the eradication programme commenced in 2005, two years after I wrote this article, and by 2012 only about 60 Ruddy Ducks were estimated to be left, which had fallen to about 10 by 2019. Nowadays any records of Ruddy Ducks in the UK tend to be suppressed to avoid them being shot and the species may well re-establish itself one day at a few specific localities.

During the last year, the organisation Wild Justice, has been campaigning against the continued release of non-native game birds into the countryside. Every year this includes 43 million Pheasants and 9 million Red-legged Partridges, numbers that have increased about ten-fold in the last 45 years. As both species eat a wide range of native plants, invertebrates and reptiles, it means less food is available for our native species, and as Pheasants are present throughout virtually the whole of the United Kingdom, their impact is enormous.

Male ring-necked Pheasant.

Additional concerns relate to the lead ammunition used to shoot them, the transmission of disease (especially Lyme disease via the ticks that live on Pheasants) and the unintentional side effects that rearing and releasing Pheasants have on the increasing abundance of predators. However, the good news is that in June 2020, Wild Justice was granted a judicial review of the impacts of vast releases of non-native gamebirds on sites of high nature conservation importance. This is definitely a step, albeit a small one, in the right direction.

So how about the impact of all the other non-native species on the indigenous populations? It is known that, at least in East Anglia, Egyptian Geese are occupying nesting holes in trees that would otherwise be available for Barn Owls. Canada Geese have spread throughout most of England and Wales, and are known to be aggressive to and to hybridise with native species, and may be contributing to water eutrophication and agricultural damage. Both Egyptian and Canada Geese were introduced into Britain in the 17th century to enhance the avifauna of the gentry's lakes, and so their introduction was not accidental, unlike that of the Ring-necked Parakeet, which also can potentially adversely affect certain native species by occupying potential nest sites.

But what about the reintroduction of species that formerly bred in the British Isles, but which became extinct as a direct result of human persecution, such as the Red Kite and White-tailed Eagle. In the Middle Ages, Red Kites were valued as scavengers in towns and cities, and as such were specially protected. However, by the 17th or 18th centuries the species had begun to decline due largely to persecution, although it still bred throughout Britain up to the beginning of the 19th century. By 1890 it was confined to Wales as a breeding bird. Plans to reintroduce Red Kites to England and Scotland were initially controversial but in 1989 the first young Swedish Red Kites were released in the Chilterns and on the Black Isle in Scotland, while the first pair bred in 1992. Since then the population growth in the south of England has been astronomical and I have to admit that I am delighted to be able to regularly see Red Kites on my birding excursions around Norfolk.

But 'reintroducing' White-tailed Eagles, at least to East Anglia, is a different matter, as I explained in a letter to the magazine *BirdWatching* in February 2009:

> … There is no evidence that White-tailed Eagles ever nested in Norfolk (or Suffolk). In all four Norfolk avifaunas published since the 19th century, the species is simply included as a casual visitor, usually in immature plumage and the majority in winter.
>
> According to *Birds in England* by Andy Brown and Phil Grice, although the White-tailed Eagle was probably widespread in England until at least 1,000 years ago, firm evidence that the birds ever bred in this country is rather scant.
>
> Therefore it is incorrect to talk about reintroducing a species that did not formerly breed. Additional circumstantial evidence is shown by the total absence of the Anglo-Saxon word for eagle – erne or earn – in any place name in Norfolk. For this reason, as well as the undoubted disturbance that resident White-tailed Eagles would cause at our coastal reserves, I am completely opposed to introducing an alien species.

Therefore I was delighted when possible plans to introduce White-tailed Eagles to a coastal site in north-west Norfolk and to a coastal area near Minsmere in

Suffolk were dropped. That is not to say, I wouldn't enjoy seeing a genuinely wild White-tailed Eagle sailing effortlessly over my regular haunts in north Norfolk!

Adult White-tailed Eagle in Sweden.

*   *   *

Chapter 14

Competitive birding

My friends say that I am competitive. If that means wanting to win, I suppose that I can't disagree with them, which probably explains why I enjoy taking part in 'Bird Races' and 'Big Days'. I believe that the first such event in which I participated was The Bardsey Appeal Sponsored Bird Count, held during the first half of January 1979. I can't remember much of the day, which is not surprising as it was over 40 years ago, but fortunately I wrote an account of it that was published in the *Bardsey Bird Observatory Newsletter*, under the title "An Elusive Winter Century":

A Sponsored Bird-Watch on January 1st was just not on! If New Year's Eve lived up to tradition, it would be hard enough to struggle out of bed by midday, let alone at dawn. The organisers of the Bardsey Appeal Sponsored Bird Count had also failed to take into account the vagaries of a British winter, for the roads of North Norfolk were almost impassable during the first week of January. However, my love of islands made me determined to support the Appeal, and so I decided to try on January 9th.

The day dawned with clear skies, a heavy overnight frost and no wind – ideal conditions for the count. I opened my account with a Blackbird calling outside the kitchen window whilst dawn was breaking. By the time I'd climbed into the car, I was up to four species, and it was only just light enough to consider using binoculars.

I'd decided to start with a visit to the parkland and lake at Felbrigg Hall. This enabled me to record within a few minutes of arriving what could have been some difficult species such as Brambling, Nuthatch and Great Spotted Woodpecker. Unfortunately the lake was frozen over and no ducks or grebes were present. However, this no doubt accounted for a Water Rail that flew clumsily out of some long grass and dropped noisily into the reeds. A small snipe, which was seen fleetingly in the same area, could not be relocated and another possible species for the day was lost. There was no problem, however, with the Woodcock that exploded silently from beneath my feet near the lakeside alders. Unfortunately though no Siskins or Redpolls were present in this their favourite locality. A very brief stop at a nearby conifer stand enabled me to record Goldcrest, Coal and Long-tailed Tits, so that by the time I had returned to the car, after just half-an-hour in the field, my total already stood at 31. If only the rest of the day could be as easy!

A hurried cup of coffee back home in Sheringham, where my birdwatching companion for the rest of the day joined me, and then down to the sea-front, where four species of waders, five gulls and a Fulmar took the total past 40. For many years, the same Glaucous Gull has wintered in the Weybourne area of north Norfolk, and so we stopped there on our way to Cley. Despite 'wasting' nearly half-an-hour along the beach and nearby scrub, we added only three species and failed to find the 'ever present' (except today!) Glaucous Gull, nor the regular pair of Stonechats.

On arriving at Cley, it was difficult to keep up with all the new species that were found in the first few minutes – Grey Heron, Brent and Canada Geese, Wigeon, Teal, Coot and so on. A female Hen Harrier lazily quartering the reeds was one of three that we were to see that day. Arnold's Marsh held the usual wintering ducks and waders, in addition to some less common hard-weather arrivals, such as a drake Scaup and six Red-breasted Mergansers. Amongst the waders was a fine winter-plumaged Spotted Redshank, whilst the flock of 70 Snow Buntings twinkling along the shingle brought home the delights of winter birdwatching.

Being privileged in having access to the privately owned Salthouse Marsh, we were able to cut across to the south of the Sea-pool and so get the sun behind us. There in the middle of the water, diving with the Goldeneye, was one of the most attractive of our ducks, an immaculate drake Smew. Smew is a scarce winter visitor to Norfolk and this was the first adult drake I had seen in the county. A party of Bearded Tits was chinging its way through the nearby reed bed, whilst a Bittern which took off only a few feet from us was an unexpected bonus. It took our total into the 70s, and it was still only 11.30 am. As if trying to catch us out, a skein of 15 geese flying against the sun turned out to be White-fronts rather than the more likely Brents.

We left Cley and set out for the saltings at Morston, having recorded several species that we thought unlikely candidates the day before. The saltings, though, and in particular the channel between there and Blakeney Point, were rather disappointing. No Long-tailed Duck and none of the rarer grebes. Nevertheless, a fine male Hen Harrier scaring the life out of the Starlings, Teal, and waders more than compensated, even if it wasn't a new species for the day.

Bayfield Lake, near Holt, proved to be still frozen over and so once again we were thwarted in our attempt to add Tufted Duck and Pochard. Glandford Mill failed to provide a Grey Wagtail, but at least there was a pair of Egyptian Geese on the water meadows. The total by now stood at 86 and it was becoming more and more difficult to locate new species. Although two-and-a-half hours of daylight were left, that magical figure of 100 seemed a long way off.

We still hadn't managed Mistle Thrush, Tree Sparrow or Bullfinch, and so we opted for a short walk along Marsh Lane at Wiveton. Within a few minutes, both Mistle Thrush and Tree Sparrow had been ticked off, as well as a Ruff, feeding on the flooded meadows alongside numerous Snipe and Redshank. A sudden flash of turquoise blue and there was a Kingfisher purposefully making its way along the dyke to a branch overhanging a small patch of frozen water in the pond by the alder copse. We followed the track and as well as an unusually close view of the Kingfisher patiently waiting on its perch for its lunch, we found a small party of Redpolls in the alders, but still no Bullfinch. Moving further down the lane and across the marsh we came upon a covey of Red-legged Partridges, which took our total to 92, while a female Smew was a surprise find on one of the dykes.

Knowing that a party of Shorelarks had been present for over a month on the beach at Salthouse, we drove back through Cley and along the beach road. Halfway along, a herd of five adult swans flew in from the east and settled on a nearby pool. A quick look through binoculars confirmed our first impressions – Whoopers, another species for the day's tally. Whilst watching them through our telescopes, we noticed some rather plain brown birds creeping around amongst the low marshland vegetation, then one turned, revealing the black and yellow head markings of a Shorelark. We still hadn't recorded a diver or grebe, other than Dabchick, and so we thought that a short sea-watch might be rewarding. A fine Great Northern Diver flew past almost as soon as we had sat down, but virtually nothing else came into sight during the next 20 minutes. No Red-throated Diver, Common Scoter nor Glaucous Gull, all species one would normally expect.

Before finishing the day on Salthouse Heath in the hope of a Merlin, we thought we would return to the old camp at Weybourne for what had become our bogey bird, the Bullfinch. Despite a brief, but thorough search, none were to be found, although a Magpie proved to be our final addition, making a grand total of 96 species; for we found nothing new on the Heath.

So near to 100 yet so far – but just a minute, how about the Racing Pigeon on Sheringham promenade, the feral Snow Goose with the Canadas at Cley, the Muscovy Ducks on the pond at Salthouse and didn't I hear a cockerel crowing at dawn? But then I suppose that would be cheating!

Seven years later I was privileged to be invited to join the Norfolk Naturalists Trust (NNT) North Norfolk and Norwich team competing in the first *Country Life*/Royal Society for Nature Conservation (RSNC) County Birdwatch, alongside team members Bryan Bland, Pete Milford and Nigel Mears. Although the main objective was to raise funds for the British Wildlife Appeal, we directed all our sponsors to the NNT West Norfolk team, under the leadership of Malcolm Raines, in order that we could concentrate on careful planning for the day. This is probably the most important part of ensuring a good species total, involving pre-event visits to sites on the itinerary and contacting local birders around the county for details of likely 'stake outs' for the more difficult and elusive species.

Of course, Bryan Bland was an ideal person to lead our team, as he regularly visited most of the good sites in Norfolk while taking clients around the county on his birding tours. Between us, we drew up a proposed route with arrival and departure times down to the last minute at the 20 localities on our itinerary. Looking back, we clearly took it very seriously, as the sheet listing the times and exact route is headed 'Confidential'! It was apparent that we were not only competing against the other counties, but also against the West Norfolk team.

The idea was to record as many species as possible within 24 hours over the weekend 10th/11th May 1986 and the challenge was taken up by more than 60 teams of four scattered around 33 counties of England and Wales. Species could be included in the total if they were either seen or heard, but all four members of the team had to see or hear them all. Therefore it was important to have a good working knowledge of the songs and calls of all the species likely to be encountered.

Unfortunately the day we chose, the Saturday, was cold with a strong westerly wind. Undeterred, our team started off from Bryan's house in Cley at 3am, although we did not start the count until arriving at our first destination, East Wretham in the Brecks at 3.50am, ten minutes ahead of schedule. Our first species was a calling Tawny Owl. Notable, if not unexpected species recorded in the Brecks included Golden Pheasant, Stone Curlew, roding Woodcocks, Woodlark and Crossbill. By the time we left Breckland, three hours later, our total had risen to a respectable 67. On reflection a detour to Welney, which took an hour and a half out of the best time of the day, was probably not justified but we did find a late, presumably injured, Whooper Swan on the Reserve. So on up to the north-west Norfolk coast, where we were lucky enough to find a Slavonian Grebe off Hunstanton, while a brief seawatch at Holme produced the expected raft of Eiders and Common Scoters, and even two Velvet Scoters with them, but a Hobby that flew in off the sea was a lucky bonus.

Our next port of call was the RSPB Reserve at Titchwell, where the highlights included the first of three Bitterns that we heard booming (the other two were at Cley and Hickling), Spotted Redshank and Little Gull. Then to one of our 'secret' stake outs: Brancaster Common, where we located the Long-eared Owl in a dense hawthorn clump that Bryan had found a week earlier. We decided to miss out Holkham that had been on our original itinerary and headed straight to Wells woods, where the long-staying male Serin was in fine voice near the toilet block, as was a Grasshopper Warbler in the nearby scrub. By the time we left Wells just after midday, we were over an hour ahead of schedule and we had passed 120 species for the day.

So onto Cley, where we notched up several new birds including Spoonbill, which in those days was far less common than it is now, and a drake Garganey in front of Daukes Hide. By the time we left Cley we were two hours ahead of our planned schedule and decided to add in several nearby locations that we had not planned to visit, such as Salthouse Heath, where we heard a Nightingale singing, and Weybourne Camp, where we were fortunate to see one of our 'bogey' birds, Bullfinch, and two Hawfinches in flight, a species that we had missed at East Wretham. Then on to Felbrigg, where the then reliable pair of Mandarins was easily located in their regular spot: the small pond by the drive near the Sexton's Gate entrance.

The long drive to Lyng and Sparham Gravel Pits proved to be worthwhile with a pair of Little Ringed Plovers at the former and a late female Smew at the latter.

Nigel Mears, Pete Milford and Bryan Bland near Lyng.

We were still missing several common woodland birds but we were hopeful that they would be found at the RSPB's Strumpshaw Reserve, which was our next location and our first in Broadland. Sure enough, three of our missing species: Great Spotted Woodpecker, Jay and Long-tailed Tit were found while we wandered through the riverside woods, as well as our first Cetti's Warbler. A brief stop at Winterton failed to add any species, but a single Crane feeding in a dyke on the grazing marshes at Horsey was a species we could easily have missed. Our final destination was the public hide overlooking Rush Hills scrape at Hickling, where we arrived at 8pm and added the last two species to our day list, including a singing Savi's Warbler. By the time that we left our grand total had reached 149 species, although two were subsequently rejected by the judging panel, probably justifiably: 4 Snow Geese and a Barnacle Goose at Cley. We arrived back at Bryan's home at 10pm, having driven 275 miles. However, this was nothing compared with the 655 miles covered by the High Batts team from Yorkshire. We subsequently learnt that other species present in Norfolk on that day, but which we had missed, included Bewick's Swan, Red-breasted Merganser, Montagu's Harrier, Osprey, Dotterel, Curlew Sandpiper, Whimbrel, Greenshank, Short-eared Owl, Ring Ouzel, Firecrest and Golden Oriole. We were determined to beat 150 next year!

The organisers wisely decided at the start that some form of handicap was needed, in order that a land-locked county such as Berkshire could compete with coastal counties such as Yorkshire and Norfolk. Each county was given a target figure, based upon those species on their county lists, which could possibly (if not probably) be seen or heard in the second week of May. Ours was 195, which meant that we had achieved 75%. Although we won the Collins book prize for the highest score of the day with 147 species, we were pipped at the post by the Woolwich Watchers team from Kent (David Tomlinson, Andrew Henderson, Bob Bland and Don Taylor) for the *Country Life* Barn Owl trophy with their score of 76.47% of their target.

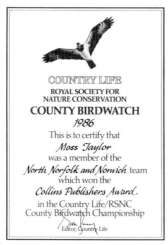

County Birdwatch Certificate.

A two-page article about the bird race, written by Derek Moore (one of the judging panel), appeared in the May edition of *Country Life*, which amusingly included the misfortunes of some of the competing teams:

…However, other teams had problems. Worst luck befell the sole Surrey team, whose driver broke his key in the lock at 5pm. The team were marooned, eventually being transported back to Barnes by AA Relay, where they started again (they eventually saw 83 species). Similar difficulties occurred in Rutland; when looking for a single Redshank, the team managed to lock themselves out of their car. Access was gained by the subtle use of a piece of fence wire, and the team went on to find an impressive 108 species. Slightly more fortunate were the Coast Group of Northumberland Wildlife Trust, whose car broke down on the way home and had to be towed back.

The Birdwatch also confirmed the vigilance of the country constabulary. In Wales, the Glamorgan Grippers were apprehended on three separate occasions by three different patrol cars. Team leader Philip Bristow reports that, standing next to a completely silent reedbed in complete darkness at an hour past midnight with a pair of binoculars around your neck, it can be quite hard to convince a police officer that you are *birdwatching*. The Worcestershire team, which enjoyed a splendid day to record a new county record of 106, had to steer through a gang fight taking place on the A38 (they suspected it was a rival team trying to prevent them from seeing a Kingfisher), and were later 'arrested' by the police who suspected them of having come to collect a stolen car. They were released only after passing an intelligence test on bird identification, which team leader John Sirrett nearly failed by identifying a Yellowhammer as a Greenfinch.

Bill Oddie presenting the author with the Collins prize at the Bird Fair (*anon*).

The following year, 1987, I took part in the BTO New Year's Day Birdcount, but as before, opted not to do it on January 1st but instead on the 3rd, and took with me my 14-year old son, Chris, and his friend Chris Adams. It was a beautifully clear, but cold winter's day and we confined ourselves to locations along the north Norfolk coast from West Runton in the east to Snettisham in the west. Although we recorded only 93 species, the list included 10 Scaup and a female Smew at Snettisham, 10 Twite at Morston and 2 Lapland Buntings on the Eye field at Cley.

Chris Adams and Chris Taylor at Hunstanton.

May soon came around and once more I joined Bryan, Pete and Nigel for the second *Country Life*/RSNC County Birdwatch, this time held a little later in the month over the weekend of May 16th/17th. At least the judges had reduced our target by four, to 191 species, but we were still judged to be the county with the highest number of potential species (again followed by Kent with 187 increased from 186). Also it had been decided that only three members of the team needed to see or hear each species, with the fourth member (me!) acting as recorder. In order to ensure that we had an earlier start as possible, we all slept at Bryan's house in Cley. Leaving at 2.30am, we started our tally with a Grasshopper Warbler reeling in the darkness on the Reserve and then drove straight to the Brecks arriving at first light. Our route was very similar to the previous year's with the addition of stops at Snettisham, Breydon Water and Happisburgh. We also decided to *finish* the day at Cley, in the hope of 'mopping up' any common species that we had missed.

By 5.50am we had reached 50 species, 100 by 9am and 150 by 8.50pm. Our luckiest finds were Red-throated Diver, in breeding plumage, offshore at Cley, an adult Kittiwake flying over Narford Hall (many miles inland in the Brecks) with a small party of Black-headed Gulls, a trip of five Dotterel at Happisburgh, a newly-arrived Savi's Warbler singing at Cley and a Quail calling where we stopped the car in Horsey to look for Cranes! During the day we covered 315 miles and our final total of 155 created a new record for any county in Britain, but we still didn't win the top prize based on handicaps. It was of interest to note that the total included 135 species that we had also recorded the previous year.

In 1988, Nigel's place in the team was taken by Dave Fisher, and as in the previous two years, we followed roughly the same route but surprisingly drove 379 miles, over 50 more than in 1987. Species of note included a Little Egret at Holkham, the only one recorded in Norfolk that year, albeit at several locations, a drake Falcated Duck at Cley, both Long and Short-eared Owls, a singing Wood Warbler at Pretty Corner, Sheringham and three male Golden Orioles at Hilgay. However, the 'best' bird of the day was a Bonelli's Warbler at The Hood on Blakeney Point, thanks to the warden, Joe Reed, transporting us out from Morston in his John Dory, where we also added Pied Flycatcher and Lapland Bunting. Our final total was well down on the previous year, at 144, but we still managed to win the Collins prize for the highest scoring team, for the third year in succession.

Despite considerably more preparation for the event in 1989, as far as stake outs and pre-event recces to sites on the itinerary were concerned, we still couldn't break the 150 barrier again. Neither Nigel Mears nor Pete Milford were able to take part, so Ron Johns and Tom McJannet joined Bryan and me. By the day's end our grand total was 148, and the only unexpected species was a Wryneck at Holme. As far as I am aware, that was the final Big Day organised by *Country Life*/RSNC, and from 1991 (and may be 1990), it was known as the In Focus County Bird Race. Our county record of 155 species in 1987 was beaten by a Dorset team with a total of 158 in 1991, could a Norfolk team take back pole position in 1992?

Amongst the 220 teams from 44 counties competing in May 1992, were seven from Norfolk, including the Kelling Krankies (Fred Lambert, John Wallis, Sid Perry and me). As in earlier years we meticulously planned our route, but this time decided to start at dawn in Broadland, driving back to north Norfolk to arrive at Cley by mid-morning, before moving on to north-west Norfolk and the Brecks, and finally finishing back at Cley in the evening. We all thoroughly enjoyed the day and although our final tally was only 130 it did include an adult male Red-footed Falcon at Welney, a male Golden Oriole at Fordham and for the first time on a Big Day, a Lesser Spotted Woodpecker leaving a nest hole in Sheringham Park. However, we were delighted that one of the Norfolk teams, Rare Bird Alert – Survival Anglia, comprising Bill Oddie, Dick Filby, Rod McCann and Mark Golley broke the record with an amazing 159 species. As it turned out this was to be the last May bird race in which I took part.

In fact it was over 20 years before I again competed in any sort of competitive birding: the inaugural Patchwork Challenge, the results from which appeared as an article in *Birdwatch* in March 2014:

> In common with the majority of ringers, I have always tended to work a local patch, and back in the early 1960s while living in Essex, I considered Weald Park near Brentwood to be 'my patch'. Most of my spare time was spent there ringing and recording the birdlife of the area. In fact the results formed my first published article, The Bird Life of Weald Park 1962-1965, which appeared in the *Essex Bird Report 1965*. On moving to Great Yarmouth in Norfolk, I adopted the dunes at Winterton as my local patch, before finally moving up to Sheringham on the north Norfolk coast in 1972. For several years, Dead Man's Wood was my usual haunt, as well as the old army camp at Weybourne, and it has been this latter site that has become my local patch for the last 41 years. As a result of regular ringing and recording passage migration, I have managed to build up a fairly comprehensive picture of the birdlife (as well as other wildlife) of Weybourne Camp and the adjacent Kelling Water Meadows and Muckleburgh Hill.
>
> Despite considerable detrimental changes to the available habitats on the camp, such as the loss of hedgerows, areas of scrub, extensive patches of brambles and short, rabbit-cropped turf turned over to arable crops, it still remains an important stop-over point for many thousands of migrant birds each year. Taken in conjunction with Kelling Water Meadows, Kelling Quags and Muckleburgh Hill, a wide variety of habitats are present in this my local patch, that is bounded to the south by the main coast road and to the north by the North Sea. Having personally recorded here about 170 species each year, with up

to another 30 seen annually by other observers, I felt that this would make a suitable area to cover during the inaugural year of the Patchwork Challenge. The idea of which is to record as many species as possible and accumulate the maximum number of points during the year in or from ones chosen patch. Little did I appreciate just how addictive and time consuming it would become!

The year 2013 started on a beautiful cloudless day, which found me walking around my patch at Weybourne, as I would do on no less than another 262 days, before the year's end. By lunchtime on January 1st my tally stood at 41 species, including a fine Great Northern Diver flying west close inshore, so a fairly satisfactory start. The next morning a Black-throated Diver swimming a hundred yards off the beach, completed my likely final haul of three species of divers. Heavy snow in mid-month limited the number of visits possible, but by the end of January, my total stood at 91 species, over 50% of the total I had predicted I would record by the end of the year. Other notable birds in January had been a Black Brant (one of the few 'countable' sub-species) feeding with the flock of Dark-bellied Brents on Kelling Quags, Peregrine, Hen Harrier and two Lapland Buntings.

Fewer visits were made in February, traditionally a month in which few new birds turn up anyway. A strong northerly gale on 2nd seemed promising but the best birds were only a few Kittiwakes and a single Little Gull. Bitterly cold weather lasted for much of the month but without resulting in any significant hard weather movements and by the end of February my grand total had only risen by another eight species to 99. Would March be any more rewarding? By mid-month only a handful of new species had been added but at least they included an adult Mediterranean Gull and a storm-driven immature Shag that chose to keep out of the wind behind my parked camper van, otherwise I might well have missed it!

First-winter Shag in February 2013.

The first rarity of the year appeared on March 15th in the shape of a female Siberian Stonechat, but unfortunately it moved on within a few minutes and despite careful searching could not be relocated. Like Little Grebes and Great Grey Shrikes, stonechats have an uncanny knack of being able to totally disappear! An easterly gale on 20th produced the first decent seawatch of 2013 and during a two-hour period, almost 300 Gannets flew east into the teeth of the gale, and best of all a totally unexpected and out-of-season Cory's Shearwater passed offshore, as well as the first Sandwich Tern of the spring. Things were definitely looking up! Over the next couple of days, the sea produced another two additions in the shape of an immature Bewick's Swan riding out the swell with two adult Mutes and the next day, my favourite species, a Bonxie. By the month's end the first Chiffchaff was singing in the lane alongside Kelling WM and my total had risen to 113 species, amassing 154 points, each species being awarded a varying number of points depending on its relative abundance and for the rarer species whether or not it was self-found.

Kelling Water Meadows in spring 2013.

A late start on April 1st meant that I missed a Grey Phalarope that was photographed as it flew east close inshore, as well as 2 White-fronted Geese, as it turned out two species that I failed to see during the course of the year. Rather cold, unseasonal weather meant that the majority of migrants were slow in arriving and it really wasn't until 13th that the spring really started. During the course of a full day's birding at Weybourne, I recorded 71 species, including Red Kite (one of five raptor species), Ring Ouzel, 2 Black Redstarts and a Firecrest, which I ringed.

Male Firecrest in spring 2013.

Several of the common summer migrants were added the next day but unfortunately I missed a first-winter Iceland Gull that had been resting on the beach with other gulls before flying off west. One of the highlights of the month was a loose flock of 11 White Wagtails avidly feeding on a recently harrowed field on the camp, although this total was surpassed the next day by other observers who recorded no less than 48 on Kelling WM, almost certainly the highest count ever made in England, if not the British Isles. New species continued to appear on most days, although two of the rarest, a Citrine Wagtail and a party of 7 Cranes flying west, all alluded me despite being present in the area! By the end of April, the only month that I visited the camp on every single day, I had added 36 new species and my total had risen to 149, but annoyingly it could so easily have been four more!

May is often a month during which southern European vagrants turn up in Norfolk, but despite visiting my patch on 25 dates, I only managed to add another eight species, the best being a female Red-backed Shrike. June was also rather disappointing especially as I missed a Gull-billed Tern that fed briefly over Kelling WM before flying off west on the 10th. But by way of compensation were 2 Spoonbills, first seen flying west over my house in Sheringham, which were followed by car until I watched them flying over the camp on 13th and a singing Marsh Warbler a couple of days later. Towards the month's end a Corn Bunting (sadly now a local rarity) jangled briefly from a hedgerow near the Quags and a fine adult pale-phase Arctic Skua flew over the camp being noisily chased by the pair of breeding Oystercatchers, while an incubating Turtle Dove was a most welcome addition to the breeding birds of the patch. By the end of June, midway through the year, I had made 128 visits (strangely enough almost exactly half the total reached by the end of December) and my species total stood at 164.

Incubating Turtle Dove in June 2013.

Perhaps not surprisingly, only three species were added in July: Manx Shearwater, Arctic Tern and Nuthatch, the last my first record of one in the area for many years. Towards the end of the month, a small influx of Two-barred Crossbills occurred in north Norfolk, but despite keeping a careful eye on the small pine wood on the camp, none appeared there, although one was seen to fly south over Muckleburgh Hill and land briefly in the grounds of the nearby Pheasant Hotel on 22nd.

Disappointingly few waders passed through Kelling WM during the first half of August, although Wood Sandpiper was a welcome addition to my list. However, the presence of a Pied Flycatcher on 23rd heralded a real purple patch and during the next eight days, I added no fewer than 13 species for the year. A four-hour seawatch in a strong north-westerly wind on 24th was most rewarding with a Red-necked Grebe, Purple Sandpiper and 7 Black Terns all flying west, but best of all a juvenile Red-necked Phalarope flying west close inshore and darting in and out of a loose flock of 15 Common Terns, which it was accompanying. A short while later it was relocated on the North Scrape at Cley. Unfortunately, I had agreed to look after one of my five grandchildren that day and so had to be back home by 11am, otherwise I feel sure I would have added several other species. Not surprisingly I felt fairly frustrated for the rest of the day as the pager kept informing me of what I was missing offshore! However, on the following morning I did pick up 3 Balearic Shearwaters and 2 Pomarine Skuas, while a late afternoon fall produced Redstart and Spotted Flycatcher.

On August 26th, a Wryneck on the camp was long-overdue considering the number that were being seen at other sites around the Norfolk coast. In the event it remained for four days. It was disappointing not to add any new species on the following day but August 28th more than made up for it with an Icterine Warbler, found in the willows in the morning and ringed in the afternoon, and a cracking first-winter Citrine Wagtail with Pieds near the scrape on the camp. Unfortunately, we failed to notice that it was already ringed. By the time that we did, we had already put out the news on Birdline and local birders had begun to arrive, so it was inappropriate to try to net it. As none had been ringed in Britain this autumn, it would have made a fascinating control.

Juvenile Citrine Wagtail in August 2013.

Finally 2 juvenile Long-tailed Skuas passed offshore on the 31st. But perhaps the strangest species of all was a Nathusias' Pipistrelle bat that appeared in a mist net at midday on 26th, presumably having just arrived in off the sea! Despite missing Garganey, Osprey, Kingfisher and Barred Warbler, all of which were recorded by other observers on the patch in August, my species total by the end of the month had climbed to 181. I began to wonder whether a total of 200 was a genuine possibility?

September turned out to be really hard work and despite visiting my patch on 28 out of the 30 days, I only managed to add four species, the best being left to the last day of the month when a Yellow-browed Warbler noisily announced its presence in the willows. On the same day, despite carefully 'scoping the marshes at Salthouse from the western edge of the camp, I was unable to find the reported Cattle Egret. I also missed Sabine's Gull, Richard's Pipit and yet another Grey Phalarope. Hopefully October would be more successful and more productive.

Having been visiting the area for over 40 years, it's certainly not easy now to add species to my patch list, so I was absolutely delighted on October 8th, when a large, all-white bird flying straight towards me from the west turned out to be a Great White Egret, my first at Weybourne! Northerly gales over the next few days added 2 Leach's Petrels and 3 Long-tailed Ducks, although I missed yet another Sabine's Gull. The northerly gales also resulted in a good fall of Scandinavian and continental migrants on October 12th with large numbers of Robins. The next day was even better when a Red-flanked Bluetail appeared in one of the nets, the second I had ringed on the camp and the fourth record for the area.

First-winter Red-flanked Bluetail in October 2013.

Over 100 birds were ringed on 14th, including a first-winter Ring Ouzel of the race *alpestris*, which if accepted by the BBRC will become only the second British record [in the event it was *not* accepted]. An elusive Great Grey Shrike was present on 15th, and it may well have flown over me the next day, but the view was too brief to be absolutely certain. So yet another species was missed, as was a Dartford Warbler at the Quags and a Pallid Swift over Muckleborough

Hill a week later. However, I didn't miss out on the party of 4 Glossy Ibises that flew east along the north Norfolk coast on 18th, thanks to the regular updates of their progress on my pager! This was yet another addition to my Weybourne list, as well as being my first in Norfolk. So October lived up to all expectations as the most exciting in the birding calendar and my yearly total stood at 195 species and 354 points by the end of the month. Surely now 200 species was a real possibility?

In the event, just three more species were added during November and all were wildfowl, but Armistice Day November 11th will long remain in my memory for the unprecedented arrival of Blackbirds. Throughout the day flocks of 25+ were flying in off the sea with many of them landing in the bushes and trees on the camp after their long and exhausting flight, presumably from Scandinavia. Such were the number of arrivals that we were kept constantly busy walking around the nets, extracting and ringing the birds that virtually no time was spent watching this amazing passage. Of the 148 birds ringed that day, no less than 143 were Blackbirds and I guesstimated that 500+ must have passed through my ringing site, based on the number we ringed. Half-a-mile to the west another observer at Kelling Hard counted over 850 arriving in off the sea during the course of the morning, so many thousands must have been involved overall.

By the end of November my species total had reached 198 and with a month still to go, surely I could reach 200. But no, it wasn't to be, I added not a single new bird in December, when perhaps I could have expected Glaucous Gull, Little Auk and Waxwing. So the year ended and with it my participation in the Patchwork Challenge.

Unbeknown to me at the time that I wrote the above article, despite missing quite a few species recorded in the area by other birders, I had actually won the inaugural Patchwork Challenge. In the final chapter I shall be writing about some of the other exciting birds that have graced Weybourne Camp in the last 48 years.

Since being formed in 2015, the North East Norfolk Bird Club (NENBC) has organised some competitive bird days for its members and the first in which I took part was the New Year's Day Birding Challenge on 1st January 2016, as I recounted in the NENBC Newsletter *The Pied Flyer*:

In recent years I've not been a fan of New Year's Eve celebrations and so it was not a problem getting up at dawn on January 1st. As Robina and I left home at 7.30am, we started our New Year's day list with both Robin and Dunnock giving us their watered-down winter versions of their songs from the garden hedge. By the time we had reached the Beach Road car park at Weybourne, the sky was turning red in the east and the lightening sky revealed a beautiful, cloudless morning, albeit fairly cold with the first frost of the winter. As if on cue, a couple of Water Rails began to call from Weybourne Hope reed bed, one giving the well-known pig-like squeal, known as sharming, while the other was revealing its presence by its much quieter, but characteristic 'kip, kip' notes, which are perhaps not so widely recognized. Within a few minutes our other target species for the site, suddenly exploded into song – a Cetti's Warbler. Several skeins of Pink-footed Geese flew south-east to their favoured sugar beet fields, while the plaintive call of a Chiffchaff from the bushes alongside the reed bed was an added bonus.

Cetti's Warbler in January 2016.

A quick scan of the sea produced a single Red-throated Diver flying east, but very little else apart from the usual gulls. The only other birds of note were a Reed Bunting (the only one of the day) and a couple of fly-over Bramblings. However, a pair of Wood Pigeons enjoying some New Year's Day nooky was an indication of just how mild it was, as was a Chaffinch singing nearby. By the time we left the car park half-an-hour later, our tally for the day stood at a respectable 30 species. A brief walk around the pine plantation and bushes on Weybourne Camp added another half-a-dozen birds, while an even quicker stop at Muckleburgh Hill provided our first Long-tailed Tits.

Kelling Heath was our next port of call, where during the next three-quarters of an hour, we were able to locate the first-winter male Stonechat accompanied by a pair of Dartford Warblers, two species that I had 'staked out' a couple of days earlier. A party of 5 Redwings drew attention to themselves as they flew west overhead, a species that has been strangely absent so far this winter, and a 'mewing' Buzzard, heard but not seen, turned out to be the only one of the day, as was a Kestrel at Weybourne Station. It was also there that we watched two male House Sparrows investigating a potential nesting site in a hole in a wall (worth checking out during the forthcoming House Sparrow survey this summer!)

By 10.45am we were driving back to Sheringham but a brief stop on the Crown car park on the seafront to look for a Purple Sandpiper proved to be fruitless, although we did inevitably add Turnstone and Feral Pigeon to our list, as well as a Guillemot offshore, taking our total past 50. It was by now mid-morning and time to return home for a quick breakfast, during which we added Siskin flying over my garden.

Continuing east we drove to the car park at West Runton that overlooks the beach hoping for some waders. Unfortunately the combination of high tide and 'hundreds' of visitors meant that the beach was devoid of birds, although the two regular Mediterranean

Gulls, an adult and a second-winter, were flying around the car park and adjoining fields, which also held a flock of 29 Lapwings, but none of the expected Ringed Plovers. Time to move inland to Felbrigg.

Walking from the Sexton's Gate car park through the woods to the lake was an achievement in itself, as the heavy rain the previous night had turned the path into an absolute quagmire. Despite this we did manage to add Great Spotted Woodpecker and Nuthatch, while once at the lake, new species of wildfowl came thick and fast. Perhaps the most interesting being a pair of Canada Geese, which appeared to show the features of the race *parvipes*, the Lesser Canada Goose, even if they were clearly feral birds. Unfortunately there was no sign of any Mandarin, Goldeneye, Shoveler or Little Grebe, all species that have been present in the last few weeks. However, a personal bonus was the Cetti's Warbler calling from the reed bed, my first record of the species at Felbrigg. I was also pleased to see a lone Mistle Thrush on the walk back to the car park, another species that seems to be strangely scarce this winter.

Another quick visit to West Runton, again failed to produce any new species, despite the exposed rocks as the tide fell, no doubt due to even more families enjoying an unseasonal walk along the beach. Although it was still only 2.10pm, the light was rapidly deteriorating due to a heavily overcast sky and with our day's total standing at 69, we drove to our last site – Sheringham Park, where we hoped to add one or two new birds and reach our target of 70 species. The feeders near the visitors' centre can usually guarantee Marsh Tits, and today was no exception, although they were far less obliging than usual. However, a bonus appeared in the shape of a Treecreeper climbing up the willow screen fence on the other side, assiduously searching for insects and spiders, making our 71st species. Could we perhaps eke out one more?

Despite the poor light we felt that a final visit to Sheringham promenade may just allow us to add Purple Sandpiper, and sure enough after checking all the usual sites, we were told by some other birders that one was feeding on the most westerly of the stone groynes, along with some Turnstones.

Purple Sandpiper in January 2016.

Our most enjoyable but exhausting day finished with a swirling mass of about 500 Starlings twisting and turning over the town, before diving into roost somewhere in the town centre. We returned home almost exactly nine hours after leaving in the morning with a final tally of 72 species, but surprisingly we had failed to record either Sparrowhawk or Pied Wagtail, two species that we would normally have expected to find.

On 1st January 2020 Robina and I once again competed in the NENBC New Year's Day Bird Challenge and were able to find some often elusive species: Caspian Gull and Little Owl at Sheringham, Purple Sandpiper at West Runton, Water Rail & Firecrest at Weybourne, Kingfisher at Selbrigg Pond and White-fronted Geese at Hanworth. At the end of the day we had recorded 87 species, which equalled the Club record set by Trevor Williams in 2018. We intend beating it next year! I did say at the start of this chapter that I was competitive.

First-winter Caspian Gull in January 2020.

*   *   *

Chapter 15

Perhaps I should have been a scientist?

In an earlier chapter I explained how initially I wanted to become a professional ornithologist but was dissuaded by my father. Strangely enough he wanted to be a doctor but became a pharmacist, and my eldest son, Chris, read environmental science at University, thus mirroring *his* father's desire. However as a direct result of my close involvement with the British Trust for Ornithology (BTO), in particular taking part in the Ringing Scheme and fieldwork for the first national bird atlases, I was able to become a reasonably competent amateur ornithologist, and so came as near as possible to being a 'professional' ornithologist, especially after retiring from general practice. In modern parlance, the BTO can take much of the credit for encouraging 'citizen science'.

As a bird ringer I naturally spent a good deal of my free time working my own patch, rather than being an itinerant birder or a twitcher. This inevitably meant that, perhaps unwittingly, I was gathering useful data from just one or two ringing sites over a number of years, which in turn were available for my own amateur scientific analysis. One of my earliest ringing sites in the 1960s was Weald Park near Brentwood in Essex and it provided the material for my first published paper in *The Essex Bird Report* entitled The Bird Life of Weald Park 1962-1965. I have always tried to combine my ringing activities with fieldwork, unlike many ringers, who have simply ringed birds to the exclusion of the simple pleasure of watching birds. This was clearly apparent in the Introduction to the article on Weald Park:

> I first visited the park in 1962 and have done so almost every week since [up to 1965], my main object being to record the changes in bird population both by observations and ringing.

I went on to describe the numbers of resident birds and summer and winter visitors, and any changes in abundance over the course of the four years. During the same period I ringed almost 3,000 birds, including 230 warblers, of which 40% were ringed as juveniles. While some adults returned in subsequent summers, not a single juvenile was retrapped, perhaps suggesting that few if any first-summer warblers returned to their natal areas in the following year.

The next breeding bird census with which I was involved was on Cape Clear in 1967, during a ten-day stay in May with my old friend Jimmy Flynn. We used 'Corncrake bones', a pair of bones, one notched and one smooth, scraped together in imitation of the Corncrake's call. These worked well in stimulating the males to respond, although there was virtually no response to this method when tried by other observers in June. Nevertheless, a minimum of 20 males was found to be present across the island in 1967, a far cry from the handful found in the whole of south-west Ireland nowadays. The results were written up in a joint article with Tim Sharrock and Humphrey Dobinson in the *Cape Clear Bird Observatory Report*.

After moving to Norfolk I enjoyed contributing articles to the annual *Norfolk Bird Report* on topics such as the BTO Mute Swan Censuses, the first breeding of

Pied Flycatchers in the county and Blackcap, Fieldfare and Redwing migration as shown by Norfolk ringing recoveries. For over ten years I was also responsible for collating and interpreting all the ringing recoveries affecting Norfolk, which were published as the Bird Ringing Report in the *Norfolk Bird Report*. While my first attempt at a 'scientific' paper appeared in the BTO's *Ringing & Migration* in 1984 under the title 'The pattern of migration and partial migration at a north Norfolk bird-ringing site'. The results were based on the average daily ringing totals for selected species trapped at Dead Mans Wood in Sheringham, for each ten-day period during March to the end of May and July to October between 1975 and 1982. The patterns obtained were compared with those demonstrated for the same species at British bird observatories and three trapping stations in central Europe.

Dead Mans Wood, Sheringham.

My enthusiasm for writing almost inevitably meant that I became a co-author with Michael Seago, Peter Allard and Don Dorling of *The Birds of Norfolk* published in 1999, which led on to co-ordinating the fieldwork and eventually co-writing with John Marchant *The Norfolk Bird Atlas* published by the BTO in 2011.

John Marchant and the author at launch of *The Norfolk Bird Atlas* at The Nunnery 2011 (*anon*).

Although while working as a GP I regularly contributed articles on Practice Organisation to the weekly publication *General Practitioner*, I found that increasingly I was submitting more columns on birds to the medical newspapers and magazines, and for two years wrote a regular feature entitled 'Out of Doors' for *Medical News*. So after I had taken early retirement from general practice in 1995, I needed to find other non-ornithological outlets for my writing in a 'popular' rather than a 'scientific' style. One of the earliest was entitled 'Sheringham's Flying Visitors' in *The Sheringham Shantymen's Pocket Book*, which contained a selection of the group's favourite songs. While in 1999, I was invited to join the team of four writing the 'In the Countryside' columns in the *Eastern Daily Press*, following the untimely death of Norfolk's ornithological doyen Michael Seago. Over the course of the next six years, I contributed a total of 495 columns, only stopping when I ran out of ideas! A small selection of these columns has been included in this book, with the kind permission of Eastern Counties Newspapers.

Occasionally topics for articles are found in the most unlikely places, and that was certainly the case with the records of Norfolk's first two Melodious Warblers at Cley in 1957, as I recounted in an article in a *Norfolk Bird Club Bulletin* in 2004, extracts from which follow:

> … During my research for Richard Richardson's biography, *Guardian Spirit of the East Bank*, I came across some species texts that Richard had started to write for a proposed book on the birds of Cley, which sadly never saw the light of day. Fortunately, one of the texts that he had completed was for Melodious Warbler, thus providing additional details of the circumstances surrounding the two Norfolk records:
>
> "While it is futile to speculate on all exciting birds one has missed by narrow margins of time and distance, the following experience brings home forcibly the element of luck which is ever attendant on the bird-watcher.
>
> At mid-day on 7th June 1957 I was just leaving the East Bank when some visitors asked to see the Walsey Hills trap, which I had left only a short while before. As we approached, a small olive-coloured bird was glimpsed flitting ahead of us into the trap. I pulled the cord to admit it to the glass-backed catching box where the first impression was of a 'Reed Warbler with the plumage of a Willow Warbler'. On checking the wing formula, however, I found that I was holding the first Melodious Warbler to be seen in Norfolk. It spent the afternoon among the foreign birds in my garden aviary taking small mealworms from a dish and being much admired by the many people who came to see it.
>
> Oddly enough just three months later, on 5th September, a second bird was caught by B.R.Spence in the same place at the same time of day and there can be little doubt that neither of these extremely skulking individuals would have been detected, and certainly not identified, had it not been for the trap. As it was, they immediately disappeared into the bushes when released, and were never seen again."

Initially it seemed that the only other information about these two birds was written by Richard in the Cley Bird Observatory ringing log: C31578 Melodious Warbler ringed on 7 June 1957 at Walsey Hills by RAR. No age is given and the only measurement is a wing length of 67mm.

Entry in Cley Bird Observatory ringing log for Melodious Warbler.

E16564 Melodious Warbler was ringed on 5 September 1957 at Walsey Hills. It was aged as an adult, but no measurements are given, nor are the initials of the ringer. So it appeared that these details were sufficient for the two birds to be accepted as the first for Norfolk, and so the records appeared as such in *The Norfolk Bird Report 1957*. However, more information subsequently came to light:

> … Amongst the lucky few who saw the September Melodious Warbler was Ron Johns, who remembers coming off the end of the East Bank with a couple of other birders, when Richard waved them across to Walsey Hills to see the bird in the hand. It was closely examined and was briefly in view immediately after release, before disappearing into the bushes, never to be seen again…
>
> … There the story might have ended, but for a small notebook that came into my possession a couple of years ago, after the death of Herber Ellis of Weybourne. He and his wife Mabel had been regular visitors to Cley since at least the early 1950s and they were fortunate enough to be at Walsey Hills on 5th September 1957 when the Melodious Warbler was trapped. While sorting out Herber's effects after his death, Fred Lambert came across the notebook and realising that it contained a detailed description of the bird [including the wing formula], passed it on to me. It appears that Richard dictated it to Mabel while he was examining the bird in the hand, and it confirms the identity of the September bird as a Melodious Warbler… No doubt the wing formula of the June bird was similar but apparently no written record was made at the time.

This goes to show just how important it is to keep for posterity original written records, a subject about which I put pen to paper for *British Birds'* BB eye in April 2015 under the title 'Where next for your notebooks':

> In recent years, I have become increasingly concerned about the long-term future of my personal bird records that I have been keeping faithfully for almost 60 years, initially in hand-written notebooks and latterly as computer print-outs. Will they be of interest to anyone in the future and, more importantly, are the contents of any value?
>
> I know of two other keen Norfolk birders who have been keeping meticulous notes since the 1950s and who share my concern – and I suspect there are plenty of other BB readers out there in the same position. So what can be done to ensure that our lovingly kept records are simply not thrown away after our departure from this earthly life?
>
> The late Richard Richardson – renowned Norfolk bird artist and field ornithologist, who died in 1977 – itemised virtually all his, admittedly rather meagre, possessions as specific bequests in his will. These included his migration records, Norfolk bird diaries and ringing logs from the days of the Cley Bird Observatory, all of which were bequeathed to Michael Seago, while the Alexander Library at Oxford University was the beneficiary of his personal bird diaries from the 1940s and his album of original bird sketches. Clearly, he was concerned that they should be in safe hands for future researchers. It was only through that foresight that I was able to compile such a

comprehensive account of his life in his biography *Guardian Spirit of the East Bank*, published in 2002.

Prior to his untimely death in 1999, Michael Seago (who had been the editor of the Norfolk Bird Report for 45 years since its inception in 1953) had approached me about the future care of the many boxes of record cards used to compile the annual county reports. At that time they were stored in Michael's loft and he was finding it increasingly difficult to climb the loft ladder to get access to them. He enquired whether I would be prepared to take over as custodian of this unique collection of Norfolk bird archives. Not only were all the cards hand-written, but they also included the original descriptions of many of the rarities and replies from the BBRC, an irreplaceable resource for future research. Needless to say they are now safely stored in my 'archive room', and have proved invaluable as a source of reference for several authors of articles on Norfolk's ornithological history from the 1950s to the 1990s. But where will they go in the future?

A few years earlier, I had been approached by the widow of David Butt, to ask if I was interested in having his records. David, a teacher at Cromer School, had also been a keen birdwatcher for many years and had kept an almost daily diary of his bird sightings for 45 years, which ran to more than 40 notebooks and another 20 loose-leaf folders. I readily agreed to take them, the alternative being that they would have simply been thrown away.

David lived at Bury St Edmunds, in Suffolk, as a young boy and started his first diary on 1st January 1945. Initially this was simply a list of sightings but within a few months it had become a record of carefully observed bird behaviour. As time went on, David began to include daily weather notes, counts of birds and reports of his excursions into Breckland and farther afield. Despite moving to north Norfolk in the 1960s, The Brecks and in particular the Stanford Training Area (STANTA) remained one of his favourite destinations. His notes made in this area during a 30-year period are a unique record of the changing birdlife over three decades and will undoubtedly be of great value in the future.

Back in the 1970s, before the advent of first Birdline and then pagers, Nancy's Café at Cley became the focal point for news about rare bird sightings, not only in Norfolk but also farther afield. In August 1975 a hard-backed notebook was started as a diary, in which birds of interest could be recorded for the benefit of other birders, a tradition that continued without a break until the café closed in 1988. When Nancy Gull (a strangely appropriate surname) finally retired and closed the café, she and her husband Jack moved from Cley to Sheringham, to be near her daughter Maria Beasy. On one of my visits to her as her general practitioner (in those days we made home visits!), she gave me the collection of diaries covering the years 1975 to 1988, rather than simply throwing them away. What a tremendous loss of birding history that would have been. Those diaries became the first of several collections of birding memorabilia that I have subsequently accumulated.

During the lengthy preparatory work of gathering information and anecdotes for inclusion in Richard Richardson's biography, I naturally built up an extensive archive, much of which could not be included in the book. This additional material, consisting of letters, photographs, line drawings and water colours by Richard, as well as his Cley Bird Observatory logs and photograph album that were given to me by Michael Seago's widow, are among some of my most valued possessions. Inadvertently, I have thus become the custodian of some of Norfolk's irreplaceable bird records. But what is the best way to ensure that they will remain as a future resource for students of the county's past ornithological history?

Nowadays, contemporary records are archived electronically, but while earlier written records can also be digitised, to my mind this is not the same as holding and reading the original material. Some of the material described above is surely in the 'national treasure' category, and eventually might be best archived securely, for example at the Norfolk Record Office or the Norfolk Biological Centre, or perhaps at the BTO or the Alexander Library. At a national level, the late Phil Hollom's family is currently discussing how best to preserve his diaries and note-books to ensure that they are available to future generations. However, a wider problem are those personal notebooks and diaries that I described at the start, long runs of which will contain an incredible amount of local ornithological history. This is a much more widespread issue, and I suspect largely a generational one for those of us who started birding between the 1940s and 1980s, or until home computers became commonplace. Unless we want our carefully compiled records to end up in a recycling bin, the problem of their long-term storage needs to be addressed. Where will *your* records go?

I was delighted that the article resulted in a couple of responses from readers of *British Birds*, suggesting that part of the answer at least, lay in entering all ones records, both historical as well as contemporary, on the BTO's BirdTrack website. Perhaps once I have finished this book, I may do just that!

Another subject that has intrigued me for many years is the all white Polish morph of the Mute Swan, but when I attempted to read about it I found very little information and what there was, was widely scattered in the literature. Surely here was a suitable topic to satisfy my thirst for carrying out some original research? So in 2015 I wrote an article for *Birdwatch* about Polish swans, requesting details of any historical or contemporary records. This resulted in reports of Polish cygnets from just seven localities since 2013, all in south-east England or East Anglia. Was the white colour morph really that rare? In order to answer this question, the following year I made a national appeal for records of both adult and immature Polish swans, by placing notices in *British Birds, BTO News, Birdwatch, BirdWatching* and the RSPB's magazine *Nature's Home*, as well as in the newsletters of bird clubs in East Anglia. The response was most encouraging, with information provided by 92 observers, including some from Belgium, France and North America. Historical records were also extracted from county avifaunas and annual bird reports.

As a result of all this information I was able to produce maps showing the distribution and abundance of Polish swans, both full-grown and cygnets, in Britain & Ireland between 1973 and 2016. With the considerable help of Dr Dave Horsley, a retired biology teacher, it was also possible to include in the paper 'The Polish swan in Britain & Ireland' published in *British Birds* in January 2018, an explanation of the genetics behind this scarce colour morph, and a summary of its historical status. The penultimate paragraph of the paper read:

> One fact that has clearly emerged from this study is that observers did not have to be experienced birders, or even have more than a passing interest in birds, to contribute useful data – a fine example of citizen science at work. Some long-time birdwatchers even admitted that they had previously been unaware of the leucistic phase of Mute Swans before reading the requests for information and the accompanying photographs. Of particular interest was an email from Colin Eaton, who had recently read out my short article entitled 'Have you seen a Polish swan?' in the letter's section of the RSPB's magazine *Nature's Home*, to his two young sons, aged six and three. On their next excursion to the Northlands Park at Basildon, his sons pointed out a Polish cygnet. Surely the youngest observers to have recorded one.

Polish Mute Swan cygnet with siblings at Cley.

Mention has been made in an earlier chapter of my involvement with the North East Norfolk Bird Club (NENBC) and this chapter clearly shows my passion for data collection, analysis and feedback. Three of the NENBC projects, in particular, have given me enormous satisfaction: the Co-ordinated Seawatch, Index of Relative Abundance and Song Periods. One of the major problems in trying to organise any bird survey is to make it of sufficient interest to attract enough volunteers, so that a reasonable amount of data are gathered. Fortunately the response of the NENBC members to these three projects has been most encouraging and all three have attracted good numbers of participants. In their own ways each has also involved novel ways of tackling the subject.

On 26th October 2016, a pilot survey for a Co-ordinated Seawatch was undertaken at six sites around the NENBC coast from Weybourne in the west to Happisburgh in the south-east, a distance of 19 miles. Such an event had not previously taken place in Norfolk, and as far as we are aware nowhere else in England, and as it produced some very interesting results, it has now become an annual event in the Club's calendar. One of the initial objectives was to introduce members to the pleasures of seawatching and to help them improve their skill at identifying birds in flight at sea (an undoubted art), while at the same time gathering data on the likely route that wildfowl, seabirds and waders take as they fly around the coast, as well as estimating the speed of flight of some of the species recorded.

Co-ordinated Seawatch at Weybourne Camp in October 2018.

Each site is manned for three hours from 7.30am and the period of observation is divided into ten-minute slots during each of which the species, flock sizes and direction of flight are recorded. For less common species the exact time is noted. By knowing the time that a flock of a certain size has passed each recording point and the distance between each site, it is possible with the aid of simple statistics to estimate the flock's flight speed. By using this method, we have been able to show that the average speed for Brent Geese is c.25 mph and that for Eider is c.35 mph. However, not all species follow the coastline all the way round, for example the number of Gannets flying east in October declines considerably from west to east, as the birds continue on an easterly bearing into the North Sea, where the Norfolk coastline turns more southerly. Our hope is that one day a Co-ordinated Seawatch around the whole of the Norfolk coast will be possible.

The second Club project is the Index of Relative Abundance (IoRA). Following a pilot survey undertaken in 2017, Club members were invited to become involved, initially with the aim of producing an annual index of the commonest species based on named locations within the NENBC recording area. The Index of Relative Abundance is the percentage of locations at which each species is recorded. The rationale behind the decision to base it on locations was explained in an article in the Club's monthly newsletter *The Pied Flyer*:

> For many years, biological atlases have used 10km squares or tetrads as the recording unit. However, this is not without its problems, not the least of which is the difficulty in deciding exactly where the straight line boundaries lie, although the use of GPS has now made it somewhat easier. The lines of longitude and latitude create totally artificial boundaries that often divide up towns, parish boundaries and even areas of woodland or freshwater. Similar, but far more profound difficulties arose, and indeed still persist, in many parts of Africa, where the straight grid lines were used to delineate the countries'

borders, which often resulted in members of the same tribe theoretically living in different countries.

But to return to the NENBC method of recording by the use of specified locations. For many of these, the boundaries are fairly clear-cut such as Sheringham Park, Felbrigg Park & Lake, and Beeston Common, but locations defined by village names are not so obvious. For these sites I have personally tried to use the administrative civil parish boundaries (indicated by a line of small dots on the OS map), as the area in which to record. The great advantage of this method is that the civil parish boundaries tend to follow the courses of rivers, field boundaries and sometimes tracks, and so are much easier to follow.

Various papers published in the *Journal of Applied Ecology* have shown a positive relationship between the results obtained from BTO Bird Atlases, which are based on 10km squares or tetrads, and the BTO Common Bird Census, which is based more loosely on locations. Therefore this would appear to suggest that the IoRA data are directly comparable with that obtained during fieldwork for the Norfolk Bird Atlas (NBA). As a result, the IoRA recording periods have been separated into winter (December to February) and summer (April to June), in order that the Index can be directly compared with a similarly produced Index from the NBA.

By the end of February 2020, the data from three winters were available and the vast majority of the 67 common species analysed showed a worrying decline compared with the NBA. In particular, three species showed an average decline over the three winters in excess of 50%: Grey Partridge 75%, Lapwing 51% and Yellowhammer 56%, which mirrors data obtained nationally. Unfortunately the Covid-19 pandemic meant that fieldwork could not be carried out during the summer period of 2020, but results from the previous two summers showed that the same three species had also shown major declines as breeding species compared with the NBA, as had Turtle Dove, Cuckoo, Mistle Thrush and Spotted Flycatcher. Of course, on the plus side, dramatic increases are apparent for Little Egret, Red Kite and Buzzard, again reflecting the national pattern. Maybe the use of locations could be adopted more widely than just in the NENBC recording area?

The third and final NENBC project is one that records the song periods of our common birds. The reasoning behind choosing this, was given in the Introduction to the paper that I jointly wrote with Andy Clarke, which we hope will be published in *British Birds*:

The study of seasonal changes in animals and plants such as the first and last blooming dates of wild flowers, and the first and last dates for migratory birds, is phenology. The pioneer of phenology was Robert Marsham, a naturalist and meticulous recorder, who lived at Stratton Strawless Hall, near Norwich, in the 18th century. From 1736 until his death in 1798 he recorded 27 'Indicators of Spring' among which were the dates of the first Swallow *Hirundo rustica*, the first call of the Cuckoo *Cuculus canorus* and the first songs of migrant birds. Recording was continued by successive members of his family until 1958, and this constitutes the longest phenological record in Britain and Ireland.

The study of phenology has gained enormous importance in recent years, for as we have entered a period of considerable climatic change, annual evidence of the progress or otherwise of our plant and animal life helps monitor the impacts of that change. One area of phenology that has been neglected for over 50 years, but which may well show some interesting changes in view of current climate change, is the song periods of our commoner birds.

Therefore it was decided that this would make a suitable and interesting project for members of the North East Norfolk Bird Club (NENBC) and this paper presents the results from the first two complete years of this project, 2018 and 2019. It is hoped that this preliminary project will act as a catalyst for a national survey, ideally organized under the auspices of the BTO, as were the three previous surveys between 1937 and 1940.

The records of birds singing, of all species, were added by members to the NENBC website over the two years, 2018 and 2019, and for the purposes of the analysis were divided into ten-day periods throughout the year. In the event, there appeared to be little change in the timing of song by each species, month by month, compared with similar surveys carried out in the first half of the 20th century. Nevertheless, it was agreed that the project had been well worthwhile, as well as enjoyable and educational for all concerned.

Finally, I also enjoy giving lectures on birds and the environment, which is another role of the professional scientist. Over the last 50 years I have given several hundred lectures, starting with one to the Romford & District Branch of the Pharmaceutical Society of Great Britain on 3rd November 1969 entitled 'Wild Life, Home and Abroad'. My aim has always been to educate, encourage and entertain, and in recent years I have particularly enjoyed lecturing on cruise ships, at the Grant Arms Hotel in Grantown-on-Spey and leading a series of six weekly workshops entitled 'A beginners' guide to Norfolk's birds' at the Simon Aspinall Wildlife Education Centre at Cley. However, whether I would have had the same degree of enthusiasm had it been my profession, I will never know.

*   *   *

Chapter 16

Weybourne Camp – my spiritual home

The history and birdlife of Weybourne Camp are given in detail in my book *Wings over Weybourne*, so I will simply summarise the main points to set the scene. Since Roman times, the area has been the site of fortifications against potential invaders, and during the First and Second World Wars fixed military defences and huts to accommodate troops were erected. In the early 1970s ownership of the land was returned by the Ministry of Defence to the descendents of the original farmers, and various propositions were made for the future use of the area. These included a Butlins Holiday Camp, a caravan park and a camping site, but fortunately these ideas were turned down by the North Norfolk District Council because the site was in an area of outstanding natural beauty.

Berry Savory founder of the Muckleburgh Collection at Weybourne Camp (*anon*).

When I moved to Sheringham in 1972, Weybourne Camp was jointly owned by Mr Berry Savory and Major Anthony Gurney, and as I explained in *Wings over Weybourne*:

> … a large number of Nissan huts and other buildings occupied much of the land, while around them were the overgrown gardens of earlier occupants. I was extremely privileged to be the only person to be given permission to visit the Camp to study the birdlife of the area, all other birdwatchers being kept off by the Camp's caretaker, Mr Storey, who patrolled it on an almost daily basis. In those early days, the rather dilapidated huts provided homes to a large number of nesting Swallows, Stock Doves and a pair of breeding Black Redstarts, while the tangles of bramble hosted up to 10 pairs of Grasshopper Warblers and a pair of Red-backed Shrikes. Understandably the huts were demolished over a period of 2-3 years and the area was generally tidied up. This included the grubbing up of most of the old hedgerows, in an attempt to control the burgeoning rabbit population (although

they were subsequently decimated by myxomatosis), hedges that had previously provided berries for passage and wintering thrushes, and nesting sites for a wide variety of species. Other important environmental features of the Camp were the extensive areas of close-cropped grass, kept short by the rabbits, but much of this type of habitat was destroyed by being covered in alleged top soil, which turned out to be nothing less than builder's rubble, including lumps of concrete, bricks and large stones.

However, it was not all doom and gloom, especially in the ten acres or so that the owners had kindly designated as the Weybourne Camp Reserve in 1987. It was sited immediately behind the low cliffs and shingle beach, and already had a well-established small pine plantation that proved particularly attractive to newly arrived migrants, especially in the autumn. A freshwater pool, known as the scrape, was excavated immediately to the east of the trees, which was fed by springs from Muckleburgh Hill. With gently sloping, muddy edges and deeper water in the middle, it became a magnet for passing waders and wildfowl.

Pool and scrape being extended in 1988.

Over the course of the next two years, several hundred trees and shrubs were planted on and around a grass-covered mound to the south of the plantation. Although many did not survive due to exceptionally dry conditions, sufficient remained that there are now many mature oaks, sycamores and willows around the base of the mound, as well as hawthorn, blackthorn and elder bushes on the top.

Newly planted saplings on the south side of the mound in December 1987.

158

In the far north-eastern corner of the Camp is Weybourne Hope reed bed, which formerly had a large area of open water in the middle. Over time the reeds had encroached to such an extent that virtually no open water was present. The water level also fell for a variety of reasons and scrub began to spread in from the south, while this favoured Sedge Warblers, it had a detrimental effect on the population of Reed Warblers. Appreciating the importance of open water, advantage was taken of the drier conditions and the central part of Weybourne Hope was excavated and the spoil was used to create a small island in the middle of the water. A small, open sewage works with filter beds, serving the village of Weybourne, was originally sited just to the west of Weybourne Hope and this proved most attractive to Yellow Wagtails. Unfortunately it was decommissioned and dismantled over 20 years ago.

Although I did make regular ringing visits to Weybourne Camp from 1972 onwards, my main focus was on establishing a ringing site at Dead Mans Wood as described in Chapter 5, and it was not until 1987 that the camp became my regular 'patch' for the next three years. In that year, as explained above, the owners agreed to part of the camp being developed as a small local nature reserve with open access to local birders, as I announced in an article in the *Cley Bird Club Newsletter* and *Twitching*, the forerunner of *Birding World*:

> For many years Weybourne Camp has been known by birders as a site worth visiting in spring and autumn. Access has always been difficult and many will remember the games of hide and seek with the caretaker, who used to patrol the area in an orange estate car!
>
> … Whilst the owner is [now] perfectly happy to allow birders to visit the camp, we both agree that some restriction needs to be placed on the number of people wandering around. From my point of view this is necessary, as I am using the camp as a ringing site, and I therefore need to be certain about the safety of the birds in the nets, as well as the ringing equipment.
>
> It has therefore been decided to issue permits to local birders, arbitrarily defined as those who live within seven miles of Weybourne. The permits will not be transferable but one additional visitor may accompany the permit holder. Access will be on foot and will be restricted to the hard roads only, to avoid any possible damage to crops, habitat or ringing equipment. Cars should be parked only on the left-hand side of the access road.

In the event, 44 annual permits were issued and local birders appreciated the fact that they could now include Weybourne Camp in their regular round of local birding sites. Two of the most frequent visitors were Fred Lambert and John Wallis, both Weybourne residents, and together we were able to plant 350 willow saplings and 30 young oaks by the newly created pool and around the small hillock to the south, subsequently known as the mound. A dozen net rides were cut in the conifer plantation by the pool (in later years known as the scrape), by the mound and in the sycamore wood on the eastern side of Muckleburgh Hill, and over 1,600 birds were ringed in 1987. The planting of trees and shrubs continued in 1988 and almost 800 more were planted, and a seawatching hide was built on a bank just inland from the coastal footpath.

Fred Lambert and John Wallis seawatching from the hide in autumn 1988.

The first rarities and semi-rarities were ringed during the year, including a Bluethroat and single Marsh, Barred and Subalpine Warblers.

First-summer male Subalpine Warbler ringed in 1988.

The permit system for access appeared to be working well until one of the permit holders parked his car in the wrong area and when asked to move it was most abusive towards Berry Savory, the owner of the camp. Not surprisingly he instructed me to contact all permit holders to say that access arrangements had been withdrawn. Apart from this, by the end of 1988 everything looked rosy for the future of Weybourne Camp Reserve, but things were to turn out very differently, as was described in the Introduction to the 1989 *Weybourne Camp Annual Report*:

> The year started well with the construction of a hide overlooking the scrape. Unfortunately as a result of the unusually dry winter and the prolonged summer drought, the water level in the scrape fell fairly rapidly so that by July it was virtually dry. This resulted in a dramatic reduction in the number and variety of birds visiting the Reserve.

Although further work was undertaken with a digger, the resulting steep-sided channels and shallow pool proved to be unattractive to wildlife. Many of the trees planted during the previous autumn died from lack of water and others were unfortunately destroyed by fire during the military displays in early September. The drought also had the effect of preventing any further growth in the surviving trees planted during the previous two years.

Despite all these problems, the year was marked by several ornithological highlights, not least of which was a pair of breeding Bitterns, which successfully fledged four young in the Weybourne Hope reed bed. However, for a variety of reasons comparatively few visits were made to Weybourne Camp over the next five years and during this time I turned my attention to the creation of a new wetland reserve on the grazing meadow to the west of the Camp. It was part of the Kelling Hall Estate and the owner, Jim Deterding, kindly agreed to the meadow being flooded, which in turn created an extensive pool. The area subsequently became known as Kelling Water Meadows and attracted not only an impressive variety and number of ducks, waders and other waterbirds, but also a large number of appreciative visitors, both birders and non-birders alike. The management of the land was under the direction of the farm manager, Henry Cordeaux, and with considerable help from John Wallis and Fred Lambert, we were able to establish a most important wetland reserve to complement those at Salthouse and Cley.

Kelling Water Meadows.

But by 1995, almost daily visits were once again being made to Weybourne Camp by John, Fred or me. Its value as a site for recording migration, both through ringing and observations increased as the years passed, and the vast majority of my birding over the last 25 years has been at this site, thus the title of this chapter. Ringing was continued until the end of 2016 and during the 44 years, almost 24,000 birds were ringed of 118 species, including 1,981 Reed Warblers, 1,869 Blackbirds, 1,821 Robins and 1,760 Goldcrests, the last three species mainly during autumn falls. A total of 30 birds ringed on the Camp were recovered outside the British Isles in ten different countries, showing just how low is the foreign recovery rate for most passerines. Towards the end of 2020, the number of species reported in the recording area (Weybourne Camp and Muckleburgh Hill) had reached an impressive total of 295. Following the formation of the North East Norfolk Bird Club in 2015, an increasing number of members began to seawatch from the shingle bank near Weybourne Hope and just north of the scrape, as well as recording birds on Weybourne Camp from the coastal footpath. As a direct result a Brown Shrike was found in the bushes by the scrape in October 2018, not only a new bird for the Camp but a new species for Norfolk.

Birders looking for the Brown Shrike in October 2018.

Although, it is not all about seeing rare birds, as I obtain just as much pleasure from recording the daily changes in birdlife throughout the year, rarities are certainly the icing on the cake. One of the most satisfying in recent years was a Little Bunting in 2019, which was the subject of an article in *The Pied Flyer* in March of that year:

It all started with an email from James McCallum on January 30th saying that he had seen a bunting in flight on Weybourne Camp, which he thought almost certainly was a Little Bunting. Knowing James' exceptional skill in the field and his uncanny knack of finding rare birds, I had little doubt about his identification, and this was confirmed the next day when he once more located it but on this occasion perched in one of the trees to the south of the mound. Unbeknown to me at the time, James had actually found a Little Bunting near Dead Mans Wood in December, and it seems highly likely that this was the same bird that had relocated to the Camp.

The following day, February 1st, I was fortunate enough to find it, once again in the trees by the mound, where it conveniently posed for photographs before flying back into the set-aside field, where James had first found it. Perhaps surprisingly, it was the first record for Weybourne Camp, although Martin Preston had ringed two in his garden at Denmark House, just to the east of Weybourne Hope reed bed, in the autumn of 1998.

Little Bunting on February 1st.

Knowing that it would be a popular bird for members of the North East Norfolk Bird Club and indeed, other Norfolk birders, I made arrangements with the owner of the Camp, Sir Michael Savory, to allow access through the fishermen's gate by the coastal footpath on the following morning, a Saturday. This was publicised on the NENBC website, as well as being sent out on the Rare Bird Alert pager. In the event 46 people turned up to see the Little Bunting, although initially it was not very co-operative and only brief flight views were obtained. A few birders began to drift away but then it re-appeared in the trees on the mound and everyone who had stayed got good views of it. That is except for Steve Gantlett who had wandered away from the crowd. He later said that at his age he should have known better!

It was still present the next day but was not seen again on the Camp until Wednesday February 13th, when Russell Page and I once more located it in a bush on top of the mound, where it's small size, compared to a Chaffinch that it was sitting next to, was most apparent, as was its short tail and black spot behind the chestnut ear coverts. Although it was a gamble, I decided to once more open the fishermens' gate three days later on the Saturday morning. Once again it proved popular and about 35 birders turned up in the hope of seeing it. I have to admit that I was not too confident, knowing how elusive it could be. In the event, it was found by one of the visitors in a hawthorn bush by the mound, just as the assembled crowd were setting up their telescopes and once again everyone had excellent views over the course of a few minutes. It subsequently flew back to its favourite spot in the set-aside field and was only seen once more briefly in flight before it alighted for a minute on top of the mound, but out of view of most of the people. Even Steve Gantlett managed to see it on this occasion and obtained some photographs.

The following week I once more found it in the trees by the mound, and funnily enough again on a Wednesday morning. It was still present three days later just before 9am and on Sunday 24th, the fishermen's gate was once more opened to allow access. Again over

30 birders turned up and exactly on cue at 8.55am, there it was sunning itself in a tree by the mound, where it was admired by one and all. Rarely can a county passerine rarity have been so reliable over almost four weeks. As a vagrant from Fenno-scandia and northern Russia, which almost certainly arrived in the autumn, it will be interesting to see how long it stays.

On each occasion, all the birders were most generous in making a donation to Love for Leo, some even giving £10, and a grand total of £249 was collected. Thank you all very much indeed.

Mention was made above of Martin Preston, a fellow ringer who lived at Denmark House in Weybourne, on the other side of Beach Road from the Weybourne Hope reed bed. We had been good friends since his first arrival in Norfolk, but sadly he died suddenly in December 2016 and I felt honoured to be asked to write his obituary for *The Pied Flyer* in February 2017:

Martin and Maureen Preston moved to Denmark House, Weybourne 27 years ago, following Martin's early retirement as a very successful solicitor in north Devon. He immediately made a most favourable impression on the birding community in north Norfolk and his sudden and unexpected death, just a few days after Christmas, shocked everyone that had the privilege of knowing him.

Martin and Maureen set about turning their extensive garden into a first-rate bird reserve and ringing site, by planting hundreds of trees and shrubs, and constructing several ponds and hides. Over the years, Martin found an amazing variety of migrant birds in his garden. Many of these ended up in his mist nets that he assiduously set up from dawn to dusk during the spring and autumn passage seasons. If anyone deserved to succeed as a coastal ringer, it was Martin, and he was always delighted to share the good birds with his many local friends and any other birders who happened to be in the area. Undoubtedly the 1990s were his best years, as far as numbers were concerned, peaking in 1998 with an annual ringing total of 3,334 that included two Little Buntings.

As the number of migrant birds arriving on the north Norfolk coast diminished, so did Martin's interest increase in moth trapping, and he soon became an expert in this field of entomology, which NENBC members will remember him sharing with us at our Summer Social. He and Maureen also began to travel abroad more widely in search of wildlife.

But there were many other sides to Martin. Although he had retired from active practice as a solicitor, he was more than happy to undertake the conveyancing necessary for friends when moving house, as well as freely giving legal advice when asked. The Sheringham Children's Trust was set up in 1994, and Martin was the only Trustee to serve from the very start to the time it was wound up, during which time over £80,000 was raised for local children who had lost one or both parents. He was also a very talented, self-taught artist whose bird paintings now adorn the walls of many of his friends' houses.

Martin Preston (centre) at the NENBC spring social in May 2016.

But above all these attributes, Martin was first and foremost a dedicated family man. For many years he had suffered from problems with his health, although he very rarely complained about it. To those of us who knew him he was a loyal friend and a true gentleman, who will be greatly missed by very many people, none more so than his wife Maureen, children Hannah and Adam, and the rest of his family, to whom we all send our love and deepest sympathy.

Only six weeks after the Little Bunting was last seen on the Camp in March 2019, yet another rarity appeared that attracted considerable attention from local and visiting birders: a Great Spotted Cuckoo, the second one to have been recorded in the area. Once again it became the subject of an article in *The Pied Flyer*:

When John Furse found a Great Spotted Cuckoo on Gramborough Hill on April 30th, I assumed that in common with most migrants it would move west along the north Norfolk coast and end up at Cley. Over the course of the next couple of days it proved to be very elusive with only the occasional brief sighting by a few lucky observers. However, against my expectations, it actually moved to the east of Gramborough Hill and was relocated near Kelling Water Meadows. Was there any chance that it might continue its eastward journey and find its way on to my local patch, Weybourne Camp? In fact a Great Spotted Cuckoo had spent three days on the camp in August 2009, and so the habitat was clearly suitable.

So imagine my delight, when on my daily morning visit to Weybourne Camp on May 3rd, I briefly saw the Great Spotted Cuckoo as it flew from the willows by the mound and towards the pine plantation by the Muckleburgh Collection. Fortunately, three members of the North East Norfolk Bird Club, Phil Borley, Lin Pateman and Russell Page, were on the coastal footpath overlooking the scrape, and the four of us were soon making our way towards the Muckleburgh Collection. Shortly after we entered the car park, the cuckoo flew out of the pines and towards Weybourne village, giving us all excellent flight views. I was aware of the fact that while on Gramborough Hill, the cuckoo had taken flight whenever it was approached and often flew away, not to be seen again that day. So I didn't hold out much hope of seeing it again on the Camp and indeed searching for it on the following day proved fruitless.

However, on May 5th, I had agreed to lead a walk around the Camp for the Norfolk & Norwich Naturalists' Society, as part of their 150th Anniversary celebrations, ostensibly to look for summer migrants. Unfortunately the day turned out to be cold, wet and windy, but despite that about 30 members and friends turned up. As we walked around, we were unable to find a single singing migrant and everyone was getting pretty despondent, particularly me, and then everything changed. As we approached the plantation and mound, what should fly across in front of us all but a cuckoo, but at this stage no-one was certain which species. But true to form, it landed in the oaks on the south side of the mound, where everyone was able to get reasonable views of the Great Spotted Cuckoo, both perched and in flight, despite the heavy rain and wind. The day had been saved!

Great Spotted Cuckoo in flight in May 2020.

News of the continuing presence of the cuckoo on Weybourne Camp was broadcast on the national bird news pagers. Despite saying that it was on private land, almost inevitably one local birder, who should have known better, ignored this and crossed the fence in the afternoon, until he was asked to leave by one of the security staff.

The Great Spotted Cuckoo quickly settled into a regular pattern of behaviour, feeding on the larvae of Browntail moths that were present in large numbers on the stunted hawthorn bushes and then resting in the trees by the mound. Despite the fact that it could be seen from the coastal footpath, the main gallery of hopeful birders waited patiently on Muckleburgh Hill on the south side of the camp, and most were eventually rewarded with distant and rather brief views as it flew to the larvae-covered bushes by one of the pillboxes, before returning to the trees. Arrangements for access to the camp via the fishermen's gate (as was done for the Brown Shrike and Little Bunting) were made on May 7th, but unfortunately the message was not received by the majority of birders, and in the event only three people were able to take advantage of this, although they still only obtained brief flight views.

As it turned out the cuckoo remained on the Camp for 11 days, being last seen on May 14th. However, throughout its stay it was always very evasive and almost impossible to pin down. Although I was aware that I was becoming increasingly unpopular for not organising access, the owner of the camp had specifically asked me not to allow any more visitors, in view of further unauthorised incursions by over-enthusiastic birders. This was probably the correct decision and was almost certainly the reason that the cuckoo remained in the area for so long. Apart from my walk around the camp each morning to carry out a daily census, it was not disturbed either while feeding or resting, which would not have been the case had regular access been arranged.

It was a very different situation to that with the Little Bunting, earlier in the year, which tolerated a crowd of admirers on several occasions, and which remained in the area for over seven weeks. Unfortunately the Great Spotted Cuckoo was so easily spooked that a large crowd would almost certainly have resulted in its early departure. Closer, but less frequent, views were also possible from the coastal footpath, but despite the distance involved, almost everyone who waited at the base of Muckleburgh Hill was eventually rewarded with reasonable views, albeit rather distantly.

After the successes of the previous year, which also included a very distant Sooty Tern that was fortunately also seen at Sheringham, I was very much looking forward to 2020. However, I had not counted on the Covid-19 pandemic that swept the world and the dramatic effect that it would have on personal freedom. Luckily a small flock of Scottish Blackface sheep were kept on the Camp and their owner asked if Robina and I could keep an eye on them during lambing, and so we had a valid reason to visit the Camp each day during lockdown. Naturally we took the opportunity to take our daily exercise at the same time, and so we were able to continue birding on the Camp, albeit in a much reduced format.

The author acting as a shepherd during lockdown (*Robina Churchyard*).

I was rewarded with a stunning second-calendar year Pallid Harrier that flew east low over the sheep field on April 22nd, a new species for the area, while a second-calendar year female Montagu's Harrier a month later provided a fine comparison between the two species.

Second-calendar year Pallid Harrier on April 22nd.

Who knows what the autumn will bring?

*   *   *

Epilogue

So looking back, what have been the major changes, since I first started birdwatching 70 years ago? Sadly, the one change that stands out most, is the undoubted decline in the abundance of many of our common birds. While watching House Sparrows mating on the guttering outside my classroom window, which to a ten-year old boy was far more interesting than the boring lesson I should have been concentrating on, little did I know then that as a 77-year old I would be thrilled whenever I saw a sparrow in my garden. Living in Norfolk, I cannot fail to appreciate the profound effect that changes in agricultural practice have had on the local avifauna. No longer do we see the flocks of finches and buntings that used to congregate on stubble fields, as a direct result of the increasing use of herbicides and pesticides, the grubbing up of hedgerows and the change from spring to autumn sowing of cereal crops. Farm ponds now tend to be drained and patches of scrub are cleared to the detriment of all wildlife, not only birds. On the positive side, however, certain species have colonised or recolonised the United Kingdom during the same period: Cetti's Warbler, Little Egret and Spoonbill, to name but three. But, this has been associated with climate change and global warming, which in turn has adversely affected other species that favour colder climes.

The image of birdwatching (or birding, as it is now known) and those taking part have both changed dramatically. Thanks to television and the popularity of programmes on the natural world, with presenters such as Sir David Attenborough and Bill Oddie, it is now no longer considered 'weird' to be interested in or even passionate about birds. The million plus members of the RSPB are testament to the rise in interest and concern for birds and other forms of wildlife, as is the number of households that regularly put out food for birds in their gardens. When I first used to visit Cley in the early 1960s, a rare bird would attract a crowd of perhaps 20 or so avid birdwatchers, nowadays a mega rarity could easily be watched by an audience in their hundreds or even a thousand. Also 60+ years ago, the number of female birdwatchers seen in the field could almost be counted on one hand, and they would certainly not be holding any of the senior posts in ornithology. Nowadays it is a very different story, perhaps started by Barbara Young (now Baroness Young of Old Scone) who was Chief Executive of the RSPB, and recently by the appointment of Professor Juliet Vickery as the new CEO of the BTO.

Without doubt, it is now far easier to become reasonably proficient in identifying birds in the field thanks to the excellent field guides and perhaps more importantly the use of modern technology. Back in the day, the first 'modern' type field guide was the *Collins Pocket Guide to British Birds* by Fitter and Richardson, quickly followed by *A Field Guide to the Birds of Britain and Europe* by Peterson, Mountfort and Hollom, and a string of others, mostly in similar formats. Nowadays the trend is to publish photographic guides, thanks to digital photography. As a teenager, the only way I could learn bird songs (apart from in the field) was by listening to the old 78 rpm and later 33 rpm records, by one of the recording pioneers such as Ludwig Koch, until these were replaced by magnetic tapes, and later by CDs and DVDs. The great advantage of videos and DVDs is that the call or song of a species is heard while looking at an image of the bird, thus imitating the sort of experience that could be gained in the field. But perhaps the greatest advance in learning songs and calls has been the innovative method championed by Mark Constantine and The Sound Approach team.

Back in the 1950s, there was a short-lived vogue for so called 'moon watching', the idea being that by studying the near-full or full moon at night through a telescope, one could record nocturnal migration as birds passed across the face of the moon. The rough direction of flight could be ascertained, and as far as I can remember they were divided into small, medium and large birds! In fact it is still practiced in the USA but not in Britain. However, in the last couple of years, the study of nocturnal migration has become a real possibility and is known as 'nocmig'. In effect it is the nocturnal equivalent of watching visible migration by day, by using sound recording equipment to capture the flight calls of migrants. The sound files are then analysed by a computer programme and each species is identified from its unique sonogram.

Advances in optical equipment have also revolutionised modern-day birding from traditional to roof prism binoculars, from straight to angled and even binocular telescopes, zoom lenses and image stabilisers. While photography has changed out of all recognition allowing total amateurs to obtain some very reasonable photos of birds both at rest and in flight. Again back in the 1950s, I can well remember my early attempts to obtain black and white prints of birds with my first Agfa camera, and then progressing to a Praktica 35mm camera and taking my first coloured slides. This was followed by a Nikon Single Lens Reflex camera with a very heavy telephoto lens and eventually the change to digital photography and the ability to enhance the digital image by using various computer programmes. But, dare I say it, I still think that a top quality colour slide is equally as good, if not better than, a digital image. Such is progress.

Ringing, too, has changed considerably since I ringed my first bird in 1960. While the techniques of catching and ringing birds has changed very little, there are now additional methods of studying the life cycle and especially the migration patterns of individual birds. Large birds, especially raptors, can be individually identified by the use of wing tags made of brightly coloured plastic marked with a unique combination of letters and/or numbers. Similarly, coloured darvic rings inscribed with large letters and/or numbers can be fitted to the legs of medium-sized birds such as waders, gulls and terns, as can leg flags. But where detailed, accurate information is needed, a tiny radio or satellite transmitter can now be fitted on birds, and it is by using this form of modern technology for instance that the wintering area and migration routes of Cuckoos are now being discovered for the very first time.

Probably one of the most controversial subjects amongst birders has been in the field of taxonomy and bird nomenclature, aided and abetted by the various species concepts, particularly the biological and phylogenetic species concepts, although DNA sequencing from feathers or droppings has at least enabled the specific identity of some vagrants to be ascertained.

Finally, mention should be made of the great advances in communication that now allow news of the arrival of a rare bird to be broadcast nationwide within a few moments of it being discovered. As well as by word of mouth, the legendary Cley birder and artist, Richard Richardson, used to communicate rare sightings by post card. On one occasion in 1964 he pinned a card onto a telegraph pole in Cley saying "Woodchat Shrike at Holme", and in the same year sent a card by post to Francis Farrow in Sheringham to inform him of a Buff-breasted Sandpiper at Cley, which obligingly stayed for a couple of days enabling Francis to cycle over and see it. When I first arrived in Sheringham in 1972, there was an unofficial grapevine in north

Norfolk, whereby news was spread by telephone. Then in 1987, Steve Gantlett, Richard Millington and Lee Evans established the Bird Information Service and set up Bird Alert a 24-hour answerphone service that was regularly updated with news of rarities, following an earlier version created by Roy Robinson. Eventually this was superseded by pagers, mobile phones and apps. Sadly this has removed the need, and in some cases the desire, to find ones own birds, which to me is one of the most satisfying parts of this incredibly rewarding hobby. I'm just so happy that I was lucky enough to be born in the 1940s and so have been able to make the most of the last 70 years.

*   *   *

Index to People & Places

Photographs of people and places in bold.

Power, George 115
Preston, Adam 165
Preston, Hannah 165
Preston, Martin 162, 164, **165**
Preston, Maureen 164, 165
Pretty Corner, Sheringham 135
Puerto Francisco de Orellano 68

Quito, Ecuador 67, 68

Raines, Malcolm 131
Reed, Joe 135
Regent's Park Zoo, London 54, 64
Richardson, Richard 2, 4, 17, 18, 25,
29, 38, 39, 40, **41**, 43, 46, 52, 57, 116,
117, 118, 149, 150, 151, 169, 170
Rio de Janeiro, Brazil 89
River Amazon 67, 68, 89, 93, 94, 95
River Blackwater, Essex 8
River Napo, Ecuador 68
River Rom, Essex 8
River Sabie, Kruger 77
River Thames 90
Riviere, Bernard 114, 115
Roberts, Langley 17
Robinson, Roy 170
Rogers, Mike 17
Romford, Essex 5, 156
Romford Ringing Station 5, 7, 8
Royal National Park, Australia 72
Russia 110, 125, 164
Rutland 134

Sabie Game Reserve 77
Sacha Lodge, Ecuador 68
Sadler, David **30**, 31, **32**, 32, 36
St Lucia, Caribbean 87, 98
St Lucia, S Africa 74
St Margaret's Church, Cley 118
St Marys, Isles of Scilly 84
St Peter's Hospital, Surrey 26
St Vincent 97
Salthouse, Norfolk 57, 121, 122, 131,
161
Salthouse Heath, Norfolk 131, 132
Salthouse Marsh, Norfolk 130
Santa Cruz, Tenerife 86
Santarem, Brazil 89, 93, 94
Sao Miguel, Azores 98
Sao Vicente, Cape Verde 86, 90
Sargasso Sea 87
Savory, Berry **157**, 160

Savory, Michael 163
Scott, Bob 54
Seago, Michael 24, 57, 148, 150, 151
Selbrigg Pond, Norfolk 145
Sharrock, Tim 20, 147
Shepherd, Kevin 31, **33**, 34, 36, 48
Sheringham, Norfolk 28, 29, 32, 36,
44, 48, **51**, 106, 110, 113, 122, 123,
129, 136, 139, 143, 145, 148, 151, 167,
170
Sheringham Park, Norfolk 29, 136,
144, 155
Shetlands, Scotland 34
Sills, Norman 58
Simon Aspinall Centre, Cley 156
Singapore 40, 69
Sirrett, John 134
Sizewell, Suffolk 83
Skukuza Camp, Kruger Park 77
Slater, Clive **32**
Slimbridge, Gloucestershire 124, 125
Smith, Lindsay 73
Smith, Pete 31, **32**, **33**
Snettisham, Norfolk 134, 135
Sognefjord, Norway 80
South Africa 27, 73
South Ockendon Gravel Pits 7, 13,
119
Southampton, Hampshire 89
Spain 10, 124, 125
Spalla Gap, Sheringham 29
Sparham Gravel Pits, Norfolk 128
Spence, Barry 149
Spencer, Bob 7, 8, 9, 53, 56
Spitsbergen 79, 81, 82, 123
Stanford Training Area, Norfolk 151
Stanley, East Falkland 89
Step, Edward 2
Stoddart, Andy 49, 119
Storey, Mr 157
Storstappen, Norway 81
Stratton Strawless Hall, Norfolk 155
Strumpshaw, Norfolk 133
Suffolk 13, 83, 122, 123, 127, 128
Surrey 110, 134
Sutherland, Bill 45
Swanwick, Derbyshire 54
Swaziland 76
Sweet, Doug 15,
Sydney, Australia 71, 73

Tanzania 76

Taylor, Albert 2
Taylor, Chris 28, **32**, 59, 119, 134, **135** 147
Taylor, Don 133
Taylor, Fran 26, 28, 64, 79, 82, 106
Taylor, Nik 117, 118
Tenerife 86
The Amazon 90
The Baltic 85
The Gambia 63, 64
The Lodge, Sandy 58
The Nunnery, Thetford 55
Thetford, Norfolk 56
Thomas, Julian 60
Thorburn, C.M. 114
Thornton, Carol 62
Tierra del Fuego, Chile 88
Tilbury, Essex 90, 101
Titchwell, Norfolk 58, 132
Tomlinson, David 133
Trett, Percy 23, 113
Tring, Hertfordshire 7, 54, 55, 56
Trinidad & Tobago 64, 65, 66
Tromso, Norway 80
Trust, Fred 7
Tucker, Andy 67, 68
Turkey 125

Ukhta, USSR 110
Umhlanga Lagoon Nature Reserve 74
Umhlanga Rocks, S Africa 74
Umhlanga Sewage Works 74
United Arab Emirates 60
University of East Anglia 54, 60
Upminster, Essex 7
Upper Sheringham, Norfolk 29
Ural Mountains, Russia 110
Uruguay 89

Van der Walt, Brian 27
van Oostveen, Marjorie 15
Venezuela 64, 65, 96
Vickery, Juliet 169
Vincent, Edward 115
Vincent, Jim 112, 115
Votier, Steve 36

Wakeham, Steve 57
Wakkerstroom, S Africa 76
Walberswick, Suffolk 45
Walker, Cyril **9**, 10, 12
Wallace, Ian (D.I.M.) 1, 18, 26, 54, 58, 107
Wallis, John 136, 159, **160**, 161
Walsey Hills, Cley 20
Waterloo, Trinidad 66
Watermouth, Devon 8
Weald Park, Essex 7, 8, 13, 136, 147
Wells, Norfolk 20, 34, 45, 60, 122, 132
Welney, Norfolk 132, 136
West Mersea, Essex 8
West Runton, Norfolk 134, 143, 145
Westleton, Suffolk 15, 16
Wetlands Country House, S Africa 76
Weybourne, Norfolk 29, 32, 33, 108, 113, 129, 137, 138, 141, 142, 143, 145, 150, 153, 159, 165
Weybourne Camp, Norfolk 124, 131, 132, 136, 142, 143, **154**, 157, **158**, **160**, 161, **162**, 165, 166, 167
Weybourne Hope, Norfolk 26, 29, 142, 159, 161, 162, 164
Wild, Peter 67
Williams, Dave **92**
Williams, Norman 45, 47
Williams, Trevor 61, 145
Winterton, Norfolk 23, 24, 46, 133, 136
Wiveton Hall, Norfolk 29
Wiveton Marsh 18, 130
Wollongong, Australia 72, **73**
Woodcock, Martin 118
Woodford Green, Essex 5
Worcestershire 134
Wright, Tim 36

Yarmouth Cemetery 23, 24
Yorkshire 133
Young, Barbara 169
Young-Powell, Mike 36

*   *   *